Praise for *Now Accepting Roses*

"I'm grateful to have had Bachelor Nation connect me and Amanda. She's been a great friend over the years. Our conversations are nothing different from this book—honest, sometimes embarrassing, and overall uplifting. A really fun read!"

—Nick Viall, former star of *The Bachelor* and
founder of Natural Habits Essential Oils

"A lot of people have seen me (and many of us in Bachelor Nation) make mistakes when it comes to dating and finding love, so reading Amanda's book and knowing that she braved through certain storms and takes accountability for mistakes is definitely inspiring. I can see why Amanda and I became and stayed friends. She's honest, forgiving, funny, and genuine, and I'm proud to support her through and through."

—Dean Unglert, former star of *Bachelor in Paradise* and contestant on *The Bachelorette*

"Reading this book from Amanda's perspective after being on a season together is heartwarming, memorable, and genuinely honest. I'm grateful that we've remained friends throughout the years and that we've been able to share crazy stories when it comes to trying to find love. This book gave me a fresh perspective on what women go through when dating and is nothing but encouraging, empowering, and uplifting."

—Ben Higgins, former star of *The Bachelor*
and founder of Generous Coffee

"I was with Amanda on both *The Bachelor* and *Bachelor in Paradise*, and it's been really amazing seeing her grow as a person the past few years. Vulnerable, relatable, genuine, and hilarious—this book represents Amanda so well. Balancing motherhood with her relationships and career?! I don't know how she does it, but this book gives us a glimpse. A must-read!"

—Jen Saviano, former contestant on *The Bachelor* and blogger at MissLifestyler.com

"There was something sweet and nurturing that drew me to Amanda when I first met her in the Bachelor House! A few hours after meeting her is when I found out that she was a mom, which was a key indicator of why I was drawn to her and her selflessness. Amanda is really sweet, caring, and a very good listener. She used to make Haley (my twin) and me mac 'n' cheese at the Bachelor Mansion. She's a great friend and I feel lucky to personally know the real her. This book is a glimpse of all the things I just listed and is like having her sound advice in travel form. So excited for readers to get their hands on this!"

—Emily Ferguson, former contestant on *The Bachelor* and *Bachelor in Paradise*

"There was no question about the connection Amanda and I had when we first met each other at the Bachelor Mansion. If there's one thing that I'm so grateful for after doing *The Bachelor*, it's that this friendship came into fruition. Amanda is one of my best friends, and I am so proud of her for getting her story out. Through all she's endured, this is the real her that many of us have come to love and adore."

—Lauren Bushnell, former contestant on *The Bachelor*

NOW
ACCEPTING
Roses

NOW ACCEPTING
Roses

FINDING MYSELF
WHILE SEARCHING FOR THE ONE . . .
AND OTHER LESSONS I LEARNED
FROM *THE BACHELOR*

AMANDA STANTON

with *Allie Kingsley Baker*

BenBella Books, Inc.
Dallas, TX

This is a work of nonfiction. The events and experiences detailed herein are all true and have been faithfully rendered as remembered by the author, to the best of her ability.

BENBELLA

BenBella Books, Inc.
10440 N. Central Expressway, Suite 800
Dallas, TX 75231
www.benbellabooks.com
Send feedback to feedback@benbellabooks.com

Printed in the United States of America
10 9 8 7 6 5 4 3 2 1

Library of Congress Cataloging-in-Publication Control Number: 2019010180
ISBN 9781948836395
eISBN 9781948836647

Copyediting by Elizabeth Degenhard
Proofreading by Jenny Bridges and Lisa Story
Text design by Publishers' Design & Production Services, Inc.
Text composition by PerfecType, Nashville, TN
Cover design by Sarah Avinger
Cover photography by Cory Tran
Printed by Lake Book Manufacturing

Distributed to the trade by Two Rivers Distribution, an Ingram brand
www.tworiversdistribution.com

Special discounts for bulk sales (minimum of 25 copies) are available. Please contact bulkorders@benbellabooks.com.

The world can't run without girls, so this book is dedicated to every single woman I've had the utmost pleasure of meeting, befriending, and DM'ing.

Contents

Contents

Prologue:
Dear Amanda

SOMETIMES I WONDER what my life might have looked like if I'd been given a crystal ball or some other way of knowing what lay ahead. Although I have no regrets, there are things I'd probably do differently had I known then what I know now. If I could reach out to my much younger self, this is what I'd tell her:

Dear Amanda,

Take a good look around and be super appreciative of what you have at home. Mom and Dad have created the perfect example of how family life should be. You'll think you want something exciting and fleeting, but you'll later learn boring isn't such a bad thing after all.

Dating as a teenager is supposed to be fun, so try not to take anything too seriously! Be open-minded about dating guys who aren't in your circle of friends. Just because the cute jock makes all the girls swoon in your favorite movies doesn't mean the same has to apply to you in real life. Being with the coolest guy in school isn't really all that cool. In fact, the so-called cool guys that didn't want to date you in high school will be bombarding you with DMs later on and you'll laugh because, no thanks. You'll probably run into someone later in life and think, "Why didn't I date him in high school?" It will be because you didn't pay him any attention back then since he wasn't your "type." The truth is, you will find yourself looking for guys you think are your type but you won't even know what that is until you're much older. For now, let your type be someone who is kind, honest, respectful, and who makes you laugh.

You'll be so excited to get married that you rush into it with someone who isn't right for you. It's going to be okay. You'll follow your instincts and do what is best for you. Stay strong and weather the storm. Brighter days are ahead!

It's just as important to know what you don't want as it is to know what you do want. You don't want someone who will always choose going to a party over spending time with you. You don't want a partner who is elusive and only shares partial truths. You don't want to be with anyone who intimidates, bullies, threatens, or accuses you, ever. These are all red flags you should learn to recognize. I wish I could tell you to run if your boyfriend, fiancé, or husband treats you this way, but I know you'll stay in a few relationships for too long. You'll work hard to get yourself out of that cycle. One day you will find real love that makes you feel blissful and safe.

You will have beautiful babies, and you will love being their mommy. Always remember, for them to be happy and healthy they need to see you being healthy and happy, too. Taking care of yourself is taking care of them. It's okay to give yourself a break. You're not only allowed, you're encouraged to have "me time."

When you dive back into the dating pool as a single mom, you're going to feel very insecure. Don't let your negative thoughts get to you. You're just as wonderful as the other wonderful women you'll meet on this journey. Lift each other up and you'll have lifelong friends—relationships that last much longer than a date with any bachelor!

Some days you'll feel the only thing you have to hold onto is your faith, and that's okay. Nobody can take that away because it's part of who you are. Keep having faith and believing in good things and they will come your way.

First and foremost, always remember: Love yourself.

Love,

Yourself

Introduction

I BECAME A SINGLE MOM when my oldest, Kinsley, was two and her sister, Charlie, had just been born into the world. Being a new parent was even more difficult with my parents living halfway across the country. My friends were still riding the party train, and I was at home potty training my toddler. I was struggling to lose the forty-plus pounds I had gained during pregnancy and struggling to maintain my sanity, let alone a sunny disposition. Let's just say my pity party was all pity and no party. This was not at all how I imagined my life at twenty-five.

Meanwhile, my ex was swiping his way through Tinder dates, becoming a regular at any bar that would have him, and flaunting frequent trips to Vegas on social media. It felt so unfair that he could continue living his life like the last bachelor on Earth while I remained chained within a two-mile radius and a curfew that ended at night-night time. Yet this devastation paled in comparison to the immense guilt I carried for my girls. I thought I'd failed in giving them an ideal household, with two parents to treasure them—the type of home I grew up in. I wanted them to grow up with the picture-perfect life I had conjured up in my head. Would they grow up to make the same mistakes I made? Did I doom them for divorce one day? When they are old enough to understand our past, would they blame me for breaking us up or not trying hard enough to save my marriage to their father?

For years, I felt ashamed and defeated by my situation. This sense of hopelessness continued until, one day, something inside me clicked. It was as if the dark divorce clouds parted and a beam of sunshine reached down to bop my blonde head. It was then I realized that, to move on, I'd have to accept that all the worries and stresses in my life were completely beyond my control. I decided that rather than hide from my position, I would *own* it. Okay, so I am a single mom. Well, I'll be the best single mom ever! My kids don't have the life I expected to offer them. Then it's up to me to give them the best life imaginable! I don't have a husband to have and to hold. Then it's time to get back out there! I dusted off my skinny jeans, got my first manicure in years, and did what I was finally ready to do: move on.

I feel like I've lived nine crazy lives since turning twenty, even though I have yet to turn thirty. In the following chapters I'll tell you about it all, from becoming a mom to riding out my previous marriage. From looking for love on national TV to getting engaged—and then getting *un*engaged—in the public eye. From preparing to throw in the towel to learning to find myself again. I will share with you the honest truth of what it's like to be on the *Bachelor* and *Bachelor in Paradise*—twice! So many of you have asked me how and why I made some of the decisions I did on and off the shows. It feels good to finally share the answers and explain what happened when cameras weren't rolling.

Throughout the book, I will also share with you my top tips for dating, relationships, and how to navigate the field as a modern woman. I'll cover beauty, style, travel, entrepreneurship, and how to prop up other women and lean on your sisterhood for support. There's helpful information for other single moms too—I know how hard it is. Through my failed relationships I've definitely faced my darkest moments. But it was those trying times that have also given me the opportunity to dig myself out of that place—and to come out happier and stronger.

I believe through everything we experience, there is both a rose and a thorn. The rose is an overall positive message, something to take away from the experience. The thorns are the hard truths and lessons learned. As we collect the roses and the thorns, we become better, smarter, and stronger versions of ourselves. In this book, I also share with you the roses and thorns that came from every breakup, divorce, or change of heart. I encourage you to accept and embrace the roses life will hand you along your journey.

Chapter One

Broken Vows

BEFORE I BEGAN LOOKING FOR LOVE on national television, I was just your typical California girl. My parents, John and Michelle, raised my sister, Carissa, and me in Rancho Santa Margarita, California. As a full-time stay-at-home mother, our mom was completely invested in everything Carissa and I did. She drove us to school every day, cheered us on at all of our dance practices, and still managed to cook a great dinner for our family every night. I appreciate this especially now that I'm a mom because, well, let's just say my kids are very familiar with their take-out options. My dad worked very hard as an engineer for Boeing. But no matter how busy at work Dad was, he always made time to attend all our recitals, coach our soccer teams, and support us in everything we did.

As a couple, my mom and dad were total #relationshipgoals. Both were extremely loving and supportive of one another. When they met in their early twenties, my dad was immediately obsessed with my mom. He actually brought her flowers every single day for months at the beginning of their courtship—my mom had to tell him to stop because it wasn't necessary! He always left her sweet notes and let her how much he appreciated everything she did for our family. My dad acknowledged the challenges that came with being a stay-at-home mom and didn't take anything she did for granted. I never knew how good my family had it until I experienced something completely different. I thought all marriages looked this way, and I knew ours was the kind of family I hoped to have one day.

Although I basically lived it firsthand, I wasn't that girl who grew up with a fairytale life in mind. I didn't prance around in a big white dress pretending to be a princess bride, something my daughter Kinsley has just started doing. I never daydreamed about a knight in shining armor coming to whisk me away or longed for a sweet romance with the handsomest guy in school. When it came to my priorities early on, I really just wanted to have fun. I was always very into dance until high school, when I became more into my social life. Hanging out with my friends and going to the best parties quickly kicked being on the dance team to the back seat. Although I did have a semi-serious boyfriend, dating wasn't super important to me. If you would have told the high school senior me that one day I'd end up on a dating show, I never would have believed you. And I never would have thought that being married with two kids was just around the corner from graduation!

I thought my twenties would be spent in beauty school studying hair or skincare. It was always a dream of mine to open my own day spa, so after high school I studied to become an esthetician. I've always loved skincare, makeup, and hair. To me this profession wouldn't feel like work because it's something I am passionate about and consider fun.

I also looked forward to taking care of my future family the same way my mom did, always making sure everyone was happy and well fed. I wanted the same idyllic situation I experienced growing up with my parents, where Dad comes home from work and we all share a delicious meal together before my loving husband and I both tuck the kids in to bed. They say God laughs when you're making plans, and I think he got a good chuckle out of me. Nothing went exactly as I'd hoped. Not even close!

In hindsight, I realize that I'd developed an affinity for bad boys ever since I hit my preteen years. My first real crush in middle school was on the cool guy all the girls swooned over. I was that cliché girl, disregarding the few nice boys who were giving me genuine attention and honing in on the one who refused to pay me any mind. I went for the same type all through high school: the overconfident kid who knew he was the one all the girls crushed on. These boys always had an air of cockiness. They rolled around in their unattainable status like a pig in mud. They'd play mind games with all the girls, ignoring them for the most part and then giving them half an ounce of attention to keep them on their trail. And most of us girls ate it right up. I sure did.

Every boy I took interest in from middle school up until recently, really, has been what I'd label a "bad boy." When I say "bad," I don't mean they're out there knocking over old ladies or robbing banks, but rather they're the type of guys who live to please and entertain themselves at anyone else's expense. You'll notice they always put their needs and wants first, not really regarding anyone else's feelings or desires. I quickly learned that dating these guys is more stressful than fun.

You see, a bad boy knows he's hot and believes he can get any girl he wants. He'll probably even tell you so. Usually these guys are slippery in their behavior and slick in how they operate. You won't always catch them behaving badly (e.g., cheating and/or lying); you'll just have a sense or a clue that it's happened. I want you to know this sense is actually called instinct, not insecurity or paranoia. Bad boys love to tell you you're being paranoid—trust me, you're not. This type of guy always finds himself in some kind of trouble.

I have come to realize as I've gotten older that my attraction stems from the fact that I'm a very motherly person who wants to help people who are struggling with themselves. I want to guide them to be better, stronger, and happier, even if it's at my own expense. This has been my role in every relationship I've been in—until now. I've learned that taking the role of mother-helper-savior in a romantic relationship never ends well. Today I am well-versed in the red flags alerting me of a bad boy. It took me a while to get here, but I have no regrets. Well, maybe a few! The allure of a fixer-upper is still there, but my brain now intercepts the temptation, reminding me the return does not and will not outweigh the investment.

Bad Boy Red Flags

Did you know he was trouble when he walked in? If you suspect a guy in your life might be bad news, check out this list of warning signs:

- He's secretive. Does he cover his phone from you when he's texting? Keep his inbox out of sight? If he's hiding, chances are he has *something* to hide.
- You find yourself making excuses for him. If you're constantly coming up with reasons or hall passes for when he acts a certain way—to yourself or others—deep down you probably realize what he's doing isn't okay.
- His ego runneth over. If he walks around with a sense of entitlement over everyone else, not only is he wrong—he's bad.
- Hot and cold. Sweet on you one second and then standoffish the next? Bad.
- Your boundaries are constantly crushed. A bad boy does not respect boundaries and he will blow over yours on a regular basis.
- He puts you down. Anyone who shames, blames, belittles, or makes you feel like you're messing up or not good enough is not worth another second of your time.

They say you grow through what you go through and nothing truer can be said about my previous marriage. My ex and I met when we were out at a club with mutual friends. Although I was only twenty, I'd been using a fake ID for some time. I had heard plenty about Nick through our friends. They gave me the heads-up about Nick's reputation for being a bad boy, pointing out that he was known for dating a ton of girls and was always hooking up with someone new. In fact, I heard he'd previously dated a few of my girlfriends. They'd warned me about his textbook narcissistic qualities, mentioning he was completely self-absorbed. Clearly, this was not a guy I should fall for. I fell in love with him immediately. Sound familiar? (Ahem, *Bachelor in Paradise*, season three. But we'll talk about that later.)

With guys who play hard to get, we're tricked into thinking if we can land him, we've won something. If you seemingly got him to commit, you'd be the one who changed him. If you can fix him, he'll be so grateful for you. This is the fantasy so many of us sell ourselves time and time again. It was this type of thinking that attracted me to my now ex-husband. I'd be the girl who was good enough to make a man out of this boy.

When I met Nick, he was twenty-five and I was twenty. He was working for the *Orange County Register* doing advertising sales for the newspaper. He was making more money than most people our age, something that impressed and inspired me. It made me think about my own aspirations and how I'd attain the same level of success. I could see us as a power couple one day, both killing it at work and living the type of life most dream about.

It wasn't crazy to think things could work out this way. In the first few months of dating there weren't any major red flags, but some things did bother me. Slowly I began realizing his actions didn't always add up to what he was saying.

For example, even though he said I was a priority, plans with his friends always came first. It didn't matter if we had dinner reservations—he would ditch me in a heartbeat if something else came along, which really hurt my feelings and usually resulted in an argument. He'd come back around, tell me what I wanted to hear, and things would be better for the following week before he disappointed me again. I believe deep down Nick genuinely wanted to be this great boyfriend, potential husband, and someday, a good father, but he was young and selfish. He wasn't yet capable of owning these roles.

I got stuck in what I now know is a classic trap many people fall into. When you have a partner who from day one spoils you, pays you compliments, texts or calls you right back, you get used to it because that's the norm. But when you date someone who treats you poorly most of the time, those few occasions when they throw you a bone mean the world. When Nick gave an inch, it felt like a mile. It was like seeing the glimmer of hope he was giving and taking back—a constant push and pull. As I've gotten older, I've realized that I (and you!) should be dating the guy who texts back, considers me a priority, and always treats me with kindness and love. A lot of girls have to learn this the hard way. I was most definitely one of them.

Nick and I dated for a few months before going on our first break. I was starting to see firsthand what others had warned me about. He was partying all the time and clearly still talking to other girls. I'd catch him red-handed texting with another girl and he'd straight up lie about it. He'd say he was working late, but I knew he was out gambling and drinking with his friends. This was not the type of relationship I wanted to be in, so I called a time-out. Within a few days, one of my best friends spent the night at Nick's house, and he later admitted they hooked up. This should have been a huge red flag, but of course, Nick reasoned, we were, after all, on a break. Back then I was naïve enough to believe this was a genuine mistake on Nick's part. I was, after all, the one who wanted to take the break from our relationship in the first place. At the time I could see why he'd be so upset and hurt that it could drive him to want to hurt me in return. Today, of course, this would never fly for me. (Side note: That girl was one of my bridesmaids in our wedding. Totally normal, right?)

Nick apologized and asked to take me out for my birthday. He took me to a nice restaurant and won me back with a few convincing words. Six months after getting back together and working things out, I found myself late getting my period. I'd never been exactly regular, but I had a feeling this time was different, so I took a test at my parents' house and, sure enough, it was positive. It felt like a dream—and not exactly the good kind. I took a second test. Positive. I texted Nick right away. He came over, and we sat together with mixed emotions. We were shocked, excited, and scared.

Nick did what he believed was the right thing to do when he bought a ring and proposed. I wasn't at all hinting or pushing for him to make this commitment. This was something he wanted to do on his own. At this point I thought I'd really done it. Everything I'd ever heard about not being able to change a man was a lie—it could be done and I was living proof! Nick

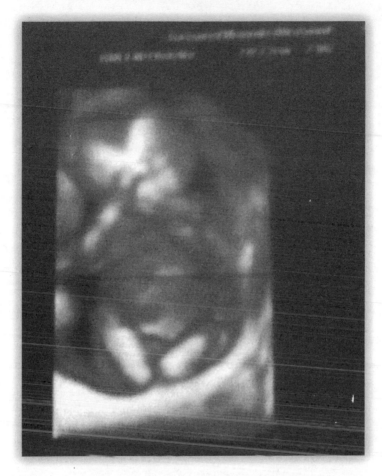

This is one of Kinsley's ultrasound photos. Seeing these photos made everything feel more real—I couldn't wait to meet her.

was officially abandoning his wild ways for our growing family. Together we were going to settle down and live happily ever after.

At thirty-eight weeks pregnant, like so many mommas-to-be, I was ready for "ever after" to start as soon as possible. I was

This is before I blew up even more when I was pregnant
with Kinsley. I stayed pretty small until the last two
months and then became twice my size!

totally over being pregnant. My feet were incredibly swollen
(as was the rest of my body). Nick walked with me up and
down the stairs of our apartment building in an attempt to
jumpstart labor. It was a really exciting time for us. We couldn't
wait to meet our baby girl!

As soon as all signs pointed to active labor, Nick drove us to the hospital. It took forever to get me dilated—thirty-six hours, to be exact! At one point, Nick left to go home and take a nap, something I wasn't thrilled about. But when it came time to push, Nick was by my side along with both our moms. It was nice having all their support in the room. I'd never held a newborn before and, like everything else I was experiencing, I didn't know what to expect. I was in instant love with Kinsley. We were all obsessed with the most perfect little person who suddenly appeared and became the center of our lives.

Once we were home, I'd just sit and stare at her all the time. I loved every single inch of her so much that I couldn't look away. I went as far as to set timers every hour throughout the night to make sure she was still breathing. Even when we slept, I kept my hand on her chest to make sure she was okay. And like a lot of new moms, I became obsessive when it came to Kins coming in contact with germs. Everything and everyone had to be scrubbed and sanitized. For those first few months, I never really left her side, though it was nice having my parents living nearby. They were always around to lend a hand.

I was especially grateful for their help because planning a wedding and caring for a newborn at the same time was pretty stressful. If it were solely up to me, I would have waited a while longer to get married. I was in no rush to walk down the aisle. I wanted to lose the baby weight I'd gained, take my time settling into motherhood, and properly plan the wedding of our dreams when I felt up for it. But Nick insisted on getting the party started sooner than later, because, to him, it was going to be one big party. And Nick loved to party.

Even though I was only twenty-one, I felt ready as I would ever be to become a wife and mother. I was done with all the late nights and carefree partying. Being a mom and raising a baby was my only priority. The only remixes I was interested in had to do with rearranging the furniture in our new apartment.

Nick, as it turned out, did not share that sentiment. My assumption that an engagement meant the end of an era was way off base. Nick's lifestyle remained the same. He was always finding excuses to go out. He acted as if the end of the world would happen if he missed a weekend with his buddies. It was always somebody's birthday or a specially planned guys' night. Meanwhile, as a new mom I didn't even have time to get my nails done, let alone hit the town with my single friends. Deep down I knew this wedding was maybe not the best idea, but the date was set and the invitations went out. We now had a six-month-old daughter to raise. I felt I had to try to make it work. Maybe, just maybe, he'd settle down once we were married.

When it came time for Nick's bachelor party, I encouraged him to go out and have fun, but I also begged him, "Do what you want to do, just please—don't go to a strip club." With his party only a few days before our wedding, going to a strip club felt very disrespectful. In retrospect, I realize I didn't want him going to a strip club because I didn't trust his behavior at a strip club. If you're with a good guy who only has eyes for you, he's not likely stepping foot in a champagne room with someone named Sparkle.

I also just had a really bad feeling about his bachelor party from the start because of his attitude toward it. He wasn't celebrating the fact he was getting married. Instead, he was all about throwing the most epic party of all time. I knew we were both coming from different places when it came to the wedding and the events leading up to it, but I thought I could correct the course by keeping him on track. I came to find out that Nick ignored my one and only request by partying at a strip club. Maybe something salacious happened, and maybe it didn't. The details of that night are irrelevant to me. What mattered was the choice he made against my wishes and how it had me questioning his priorities when it came to me. It made me wonder, *Does he really care about how I feel?*

The wedding planning and the bachelor party were really the first blaringly bad signs after we got engaged. Before, things were not great, but nothing had occurred to make me question our compatibility. Still, I didn't have much time to react to the strip club saga because our wedding was just two days after the bachelor party. We were hosting out-of-town guests and had to get ready for the next event. There wasn't time for us to fight about his blatant disregard for my feelings.

The following night, we had a stunning rehearsal dinner at what used to be the St. Regis in Dana Point. On the surface, it was everything any bride could ask for—a glamorous beachside resort under the glittering sky. It was beautiful. The only thorn in my side was my fiancé, whose priority was to party with his friends rather than focus on his bride-to-be. Nick got so wasted it was humiliating. I was beyond embarrassed by how loud and obnoxious he was acting in front of my friends and family. I'd assume most brides feel bittersweet about the tradition of spending the night before their wedding apart from their partner, but I was ecstatic to be going home with my sister and our friends.

That night, I confided in my sister, "I don't think we are going to last." She also admitted she didn't feel I should be marrying him. She urged me to tell Mom and Dad, but I said no, I just had to go through with it.

I knew all along that getting married to Nick wasn't right but remained hopeful every step of the way that things would change. Everything happened so fast—before I knew it, there we were on the eve of my wedding. At first, I felt embarrassed because we'd already made the announcement about our engagement. Then I felt guilty because our parents had put in money for a wedding. Later, I felt horrible because people had booked their flights. At a certain point, getting a divorce later on sounded like less of an embarrassment than making every- one change their plans had I just called off the wedding. My advice to anyone in this situation is not to do what I did. Now I'd take calling off a wedding over going through a divorce any day. Follow your gut and be realistic. If you hear a voice in the back of your head, listen to it. It never gets easier, in my experi- ence. The longer you drag something out, the harder it will be to call it quits.

As I walked down the aisle, the magic of it all took over. The questions and concerns screaming through my body qui- eted down. My heart melted when I saw baby Kins so cute as our flower girl. The whole scene was right out of a bridal magazine; it was all so romantic and beautiful. When Nick and I locked eyes, I could see he was crying. I thought, *Maybe he really does love me. It is possible I'm wrong about everything. Maybe, just maybe, we will be okay.*

Despite the rocky start, our marriage was good for a little while. We loved our adorable little Kinsley and enjoyed watching her grow. But as soon as Nick got the itch to start going out again, things quickly went downhill. He was always out with his friends drinking or "working late." I was always home alone with the baby. Nick and I started fighting—a lot. As if our relationship didn't have enough issues, Nick thought it would be best for us to move in with his parents for a few months to save money to buy a house. We didn't have the closest relationship with his parents. He didn't have the same connection with them as I did to mine. Additionally, his parents gave me a hard time about wanting to be a stay-at-home mom. They'd make jabs about me staying home and not doing anything all day. Nick made a decent living selling advertising, and after doing the math we figured the money I'd make working would go straight into daycare. I would much rather be taking care of Kinsley.

So, even though I knew this would be a bad decision for us, we still moved in with his family. This didn't change Nick's lifestyle choices. He was still going out late and leaving me at home, but this time it wasn't even our home. I was so uncomfortable and unhappy at this point in my marriage that I moved with Kinsley back home to my parents. I was seriously contemplating divorce for about two weeks when Mother's Day came around. Nick stopped by my parents' house with a bouquet of flowers and a bunch of charm. He promised me we were going to start fresh and get a brand-new place together. Things would be different now. And just like that, I was sucked back in. We moved back in together and, two days later, I learned I was pregnant with Charlie.

I'm not going to lie and say the first two words that came to mind weren't "oh" and "shit." We were not in a good place in terms of our marriage. We were actually in a really bad place. I had my suspicions Nick wanted to get me pregnant thinking I'd be less likely to leave him if we had another baby. He didn't want to be "the divorced guy"—it wasn't great for his image. Typically, the cliché is of a woman trying to manipulate a pregnancy to keep a marriage intact, but in my case I'm pretty sure it was the other way around. And it worked. I didn't want to be a single and pregnant mother living with her mom and dad. Even though growing up I had no interest in the fairytale family life, I wanted one now. I put up with his shenanigans and tried my best to carry on.

Looking back on our relationship, I never felt emotionally safe with Nick. My imagination was constantly running wild: *Who is he really with? What's her name? What are they up to?* Often Nick would not come home from partying until the next day, claiming he fell asleep on the couch of one of his friends. He'd sometimes sit in the car alone and talk on the phone for an hour at a time. On top of that he was working out more than ever, making it seem as if he cared more about

Charlie was the best surprise I could have ever received. Because
it was my second pregnancy, I felt so much more prepared!

what he looked like than he did about spending time with
Kinsley and me. I knew something shady was going on, but
I didn't know exactly what. My gut was telling me Nick was
up to no good, but I never had tangible evidence. Any time I
would mention feeling like something wasn't right or question his behavior, he would call me crazy. I started to believe

maybe I was just crazy and paranoid. To make matters worse for me, my parents found out they'd soon be relocating to St. Louis for my dad's job. My safety net should things with Nick go awry again was gone.

My being a stay-at-home mom was a constant point of contention, but that's the arrangement we'd agreed on. We weren't under financial stress and I wasn't exactly sitting at the spa all day—being a mom truly is a job in its own right. Nick would come home and give me a hard time by pressing me, "What did you do all day?" He at least got to have lunch with adults. Meanwhile, I had three days of baby food in my hair because I didn't have time to shower. I've had jobs and I've been a mom, and, let me tell you, being a mom is so much harder than working any nine-to-five. It really can make you crazy sometimes. My mom was a stay-at-home mom and I remember my dad was always so appreciative. Even when he came home from work, he wanted to help out by giving my sister and me a bath and putting us to bed. Having had such an involved father growing up made me realize the situation I'd committed to wasn't only not what I was used to—it wasn't what I wanted.

Things really came to a halt the night I went into labor with Charlie. Nick had big plans to go to a party that evening. I would have gone because I was also invited, but Nick suggested I stay home. *Fine*, I thought. Whatever. I was so over being pregnant. At full term, I just wanted her out already. As silly as it sounds, I decided I would walk myself into labor. I waddled my way to the treadmill, stepped onto the track, and hit go. I pumped my arms and propelled myself along. The

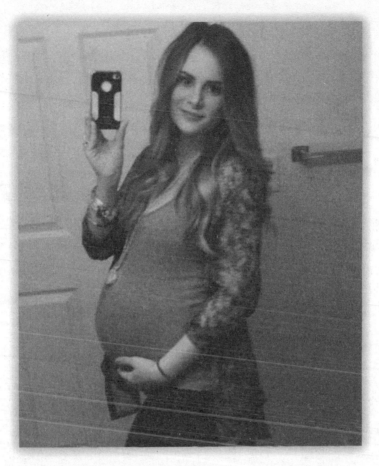

This was a really stressful time in my life, but I tried to enjoy every bit of pregnancy I could. As long as Char was healthy, I was happy.

more I walked, the madder I got. What kind of man leaves his super pregnant wife at home to party with his friends? And what kind of woman puts up with it?

To my complete surprise, my contractions started right then and there. The contractions were close enough together that I knew it was time. This was happening! I called Nick over and over again as I made my way around the apartment. Each call went straight to voicemail. I sat on the couch with my hospital bag waiting for him to return my calls or texts. I really didn't want to go to the hospital alone. A knight in shining armor sounded really good right about now. Thankfully, my mom had flown back a few days earlier, anticipating I'd need her help with Kinsley after the baby was born. I called, and she came to my rescue. It wasn't exactly the same as my man whisking me off my feet, but at this point whisking me to the hospital would have to do. My in-laws came for Kinsley, and my mom drove me to the hospital. I remember thinking, *This really sucks. This is not good enough.*

Eventually someone got ahold of Nick. When he arrived at the hospital, he was sloppy and wasted, reeking of alcohol. I remember the nurses kept looking at me to see my reaction. They could tell I was flustered and upset. While I was waiting for my epidural, Nick made a call to his brother, slurring his words and being obnoxiously loud, asking him to bring him a burger and fries. The nurses couldn't believe the audacity of this jerk husband ordering food in front of his fragile wife—when you're in labor, you can't eat or drink anything. I appreciated their sympathy. It felt nice for a change.

When the epidural arrived—for those of you who don't know, this is administered by a terrifying needle, and it's a scary moment for every mom—I was lying there alone, staring at him, trying to get him to make eye contact with me, but he was too busy ordering his burger to even look my way. My mom stepped in as always to hold my hand and offer the comfort and support I was lacking. About an hour later, Nick had eaten his dinner and was passed out on the couch in my hospital room. I was fuming. I wanted him out. I didn't need him snoring on my couch in a drunken stupor. I needed him to have my back.

The sun came up, and I still hadn't given birth. They told me it would probably be a few more hours. The very second Nick left the hospital to go home for a shower is when I realized that I was done with him. Showing up drunk, eating in front of me, not holding my hand when I'm scared—all bad things. But leaving me there? When his daughter could be born at any moment? That sealed the deal. I wasn't surprised when two days later, the day we got home from the hospital, he left me with a brand-new infant and toddler to celebrate his birthday. At that point it was par for the course. Since my parents had long since moved to St. Louis, I didn't have the option to move back in with them this time. Luckily, my generous aunt invited the girls and me to stay with her for a few months while I figured out our next move.

While I was moving, I grabbed an unused laundry basket stashed in the closet to throw some clothes in. In it I found a few miscellaneous items, including a phone I'd never seen before. As far as I knew it wasn't his nor mine. Now, when you have a big breakup there's always that moment you wonder, *Did I do the right thing by leaving?* I believe this phone was the universe's way of saying, "YES, GIRL." I turned the mystery phone on and, lo and behold, there were the answers I needed to every night spent on "a friend's couch" or taking calls from the car. In addition to inappropriate texts from many, many girls, including Nick's ex with whom he'd apparently hung out right when Charlie was born, there were naked pictures of many girls, as well as my husband's numerous dating app profiles. The kicker was his Tinder profile picture—a photo of our family with me cropped out. Nick claimed to be a loving, single father. Ouch.

To this day, despite the dating profiles and text messages, my ex claims he never cheated on me and swears there was only ever one kiss between him and his ex-girlfriend while we were married. Let's just pretend for a second we believe him. That doesn't mean he didn't cheat. Secretly talking to your ex-girlfriend, let alone kissing, is cheating, period. Being on a dating app when you have a pregnant wife at home is cheating, period. Abandoning the person you made vows to love and honor is cheating, period.

The demise of Nick and Amanda was a slow-motion stumble that took six months to crash. My parents generously helped me secure a cute apartment in Orange County for me and the girls. A friend of mine got me into a multilevel marketing job I could do even as a full-time stay-at-home mom. The job helped me keep afloat with rent and groceries, but my parents still had to help us out quite a bit. Things were especially tight since Nick, who made the money and controlled the finances during our marriage, depleted our mutual account.

Despite his cutting me off, I tried to keep things as civil as possible. Nick would come in and out of our lives. Sometimes it was good, but mostly it was bad. He would taunt me with words like, "You're a mother of two. You don't have a job. Nobody is going to want a single mom of two young kids." He assured me men would see me as used and damaged goods, plus baggage. It seemed the only option was to be alone forever if I ever divorced my husband. I suspect a lot of people feel that's true for them. I thought it might be for me. But I got to a point where I figured even if it was true, I'd rather be alone than with someone who makes me so unhappy. I was married, but I was lonely. And being alone is by far less miserable than being with someone who makes you feel lonely.

Eventually, I mustered up the strength and courage to officially divorce Nick on paper and in life. About six months later, I started to believe perhaps my ex was right. I could very well end up single and alone forever. It was during that moment of doubt when I got a call from the casting director for *The Bachelor*.

The Rose: Look for the Lesson

Going through a divorce at twenty-four was a huge loss, so I try to look at what I gained (besides two gorgeous, sweet girls!). My marriage shined the light on what I *do* want in a relationship, which is equally as important as knowing what I don't want. When it comes to romantic partners, first and foremost I want to be with someone who has the same values and morals as me, which is especially important when it comes to someone with whom you're going to have children. When I got married, I was so young and inexperienced I didn't understand the importance of shared values and morals. From day one, Nick and I weren't on the same page. We weren't even reading the same book. This was a huge lesson for me.

One of my favorite practices I've learned since then is listing my most regarded morals and values. When I meet someone new, I consult my list to see if this person shares the same beliefs I do. Do they agree that omitting truth is the same thing as lying? Are they kind to service people? Do they also think it's not okay to speak poorly about their friends?

What's on your list of values? Can the same be said about your partner or crush? If you're currently dating, definitely use this tool to decide whether or not someone shares the same moral code as you.

The Thorns

- If someone makes you feel insecure or paranoid, it's a red flag. Sure, you might actually be insecure, but the right person will go out of their way to make you feel emotionally safe.
- If you have a bad feeling about something, don't let it drag on. I didn't call off our wedding because the invitations had been sent out. What followed was much harder to reverse.
- Where there's smoke, there's fire. In my experience rumors are usually linked to truths, even if only in a small way. I unknowingly brushed off so many warning signs my ex wasn't being faithful when I should have further investigated them instead.

- Have a limit. I used to forgive and forget over and over again. This has since changed, especially now that I'm a mom. Nobody has time for nonsense!
- Trust and follow your instincts, always.
- Someone who cares about you will care about how you feel. They will not abandon you when you need them. They will not hurt you with words. They will not intentionally hurt you, period.
- Always remember you're much stronger than anyone else knows.
- Be careful about sending nudes to the guy you're talking to online. His wife will probably see them.

Chapter Two

Season Twenty

O NCE MY MARRIAGE was in the rearview window, dating was not even close to being on my radar. Kinsley was a curious toddler and I was still breastfeeding Charlie. Suffice it to say, my hands were full. It was just the three of us girls, and we needed to be there for each other. Besides, all I cared about was raising these girls to the best of my ability. Anything else would be extra and, for now, extra could wait. "Extra" included my love of the guilty pleasure television. Since becoming a mom, watching anything for entertainment wasn't really an option for me unless it involved cartoons or singing puppets. I'd seen a few episodes of *The Bachelor* before, but only here and there. It would be a while before I knew a Bachelor Nation even existed.

One day, six months into the single life, the girls were napping when I received a phone call from a Los Angeles area code. I figured it was the wrong number and let it go to voicemail. When I got around to listening to it, I thought for sure I'd been pranked.

"Hi, this is Scott with ABC's *The Bachelor*. We received your submission and we are wondering since you're local if you wouldn't mind coming in for an interview?"

Immediately I sent a group text to my friends. Everyone responded saying things like "It wasn't me" or "Wish it was my idea." Who would have done this? Could it be for real? There was only one way to find out. Though skeptical at first, I returned the casting director's call. Sure enough, it was the real thing! I couldn't wait to tell my mom, who was a longtime fan of the show. It turned out it was my own mother who had put me up for *The Bachelor*. She'd later explain that when she called the casting number they aired at the end of the show, she didn't really think it would turn into an actual interview.

Mom flew out to Orange County right away to watch the girls so I could get myself ready and go meet with casting directors in L.A. She was so happy at the prospect of me finding happiness that she was willing to do anything at that point. For my part, I couldn't believe I was even entertaining the idea of auditioning to be on *The Bachelor*. I was newly single. I hadn't been on a single date since getting divorced. And I had two babies at home. Getting me out the door definitely took some convincing, especially from my mom. The idea of being on TV alone was scary to me. Follow that up with dating and competing with other girls—all of it was uncharted territory to me. Plus, my self-esteem wasn't exactly at a high. I didn't think getting chosen would ever happen, not to me.

Still, I got my first manicure in years, squeezed into my skinny jeans, and went for it because although 99 percent of my mind was saying I would never get chosen, I was clinging to the 1 percent thought that maybe, just maybe, I would.

To prepare for my interview I went online to research the casting process. My experience turned out to be unlike anyone else's I'd read about. There wasn't much of a process at all. They asked me a ton of questions about what type of partner I was looking for and what my fears in life were. Between the in-person questions and the written questionnaires, I must have answered 2,000 questions about myself. Casting assistants took several pictures of me and sent me home with a list of photos I needed to take for them (full body, half body, side profile, and so on). I know they ask others for video, too, but that wasn't requested of me.

Right away the casting directors told me to find a sitter for September, when we'd begin filming. That was just three months away. It all seemed very definitive, like when you go for a job interview and they show you where your office will be. I returned home to my quiet life with the girls and lived as if the interview never happened. A few months went by, and I hadn't heard from anyone with the show. I wondered if they'd forgotten about me or simply changed their minds. Then August came around and the production team finally reached out to request I attend a big event called "Casting Weekend" in Los Angeles.

I was told there were about a hundred girls at the event, but I never saw any of the other potential cast members. Each of us was checked into our own hotel room until we were picked up and escorted to the various rooms where production met with us. In our individual hotel rooms, we were allowed to order room service or anything else we needed. The show staff was really nice, offering snacks and making sure we were comfortable.

Being shuttled into the production rooms made me nervous because I like to know what to expect, and during this process I felt blind. In these rooms, producers gave us background tests and STD screenings, had us talk to a therapist, and so on—all within a very busy day of shuttling from room to room. I had so many questions that went unanswered. What are the other girls like? Who is the Bachelor? I left knowing that only twenty-five girls would be chosen and within a week they'd call to let us know if we'd officially been cast for the show. This was two weeks before shooting began. Talk about nerve-racking!

I left the initial interview fairly confident I'd made it onto the show based on their insistence I get a babysitter for filming months. But when I left casting weekend, their attitude was more, "Hopefully we'll see you soon." I began to question whether or not they'd changed their mind about me. Did I not give them the answers they wanted to hear this time? Had I said something wrong? Even though I wasn't dying to get on the show, I didn't want to be denied, either.

I was in the kitchen with my mom when I received the call from producers to confirm my casting. While I was very excited, nobody was more excited than Mom! She was over the moon. Production sent me a packing list and instructed me to watch "After the Final Rose" the following day to see who the new Bachelor would be. When I found out Ben Higgins was the Bachelor for season twenty, I was really excited. I'd caught myself up on the show and gotten familiar with some of the potential candidates. Ben seemed like such a sweet, down-to-earth, normal guy. The kind of guy I should have married in the first place.

Suddenly I was extremely nervous. It had now been nine months of being single, and I still hadn't been on a single date. The last date I went on was when I was twenty, with my former husband. Now here I was at twenty-five with two little ones in tow. In my heart I wanted Ben to see I was a good, solid woman with so much to give. Hopefully he'd see what a devoted mother I was and what a loving wife I could be. I wholeheartedly believed I was going into the show for all the right reasons. I genuinely wanted to find true love. Unlike many, I wasn't looking to be famous or anything like that. I didn't even think about the opportunities that came along with being on a show like *The Bachelor*. Since my divorce I had little confidence in myself, and because my ex had me convinced nobody would want me with all my baggage, I never thought someone as wholesome as Ben would be interested in me. I fully expected to be sent home on the first night. But still, I had a teeny tiny glimmer of hope that maybe I could be the one for Ben—and he the one for me. How cool would that be?

It only took a hot minute for my ex to find out about my participation on the show. He took the opportunity to remind me how stupid I was to think anyone would ever want a divor-cée with two young kids. Yet his meanness paled in compari-son to the anxiety I faced when it came to being away from my girls. I was convinced I'd be home in a week and, still, this seemed like forever. When the driver hired by the show came to pick me up I was very close to backing out. Thank goodness my mom was like, "You'd better get in that car."

The car took me to a hotel in Malibu, which might sound like the beginning of a great vacation, but it was actually any-thing but. For the first few nights, we all were locked in our own rooms alone without keys so that we wouldn't be tempted to sneak out and potentially meet each other. We had surren-dered our cell phones early on and the in-room phones weren't connected. All we could do was order room service, watch tele-vision, and wait.

On the night we got to meet Ben for the first time, a handler came to get us one by one. They put us in different corners of the hotel lobby, each of us facing a wall, before we were called to the limousines that would bring us to the house. I realized I was in the first limo because the sun was just going down and I knew this scene was always shot at night. In the limo with me were Caila, Jamie, Lauren, and Jessica, a girl who'd be sent home that night. We were instructed not to talk about anything other than our excitement about Ben. That's why we sounded so giddy in the car; it was literally all we could say or do. The producers would rather have our getting-to-know-each-other conversations during the cocktail hour at the house.

I was assigned to a room with Lace, Emily, Haley, and Jubilee. For the most part the girls on our season were extremely generous. Throughout taping we all shared a lot of things, including clothes, accessories, and anything else someone might have forgotten. The twins, Emily and Haley, were sweet about doing girls' hair and makeup, and Lauren B. was so great with other people's eyebrows we called her makeshift station "Lauren's Brow Bar." Of course, in many gatherings of ladies there is usually someone who doesn't do so well in all-girl scenarios. For our season that was Olivia. She was a bit of a misfit who didn't play well with others. But for the rest of us, we bonded and remain really close. I became instant best friends with Lauren B. Our eerily similar personalities clicked and we had so much in common. It's hard not to deeply connect with people with whom you share so much time and personal space. Especially on a show like *The Bachelor*, we were all in it together, 24/7.

It wasn't only the girls who grew close to one another. The producers were also with us around the clock. I've heard cast members say things about the producers such as, "I thought the producers were my friends and they really weren't." I've heard people talk about how manipulative and cruel they can be. Personally, I don't really feel that way. I understand their job is obviously to produce good television, but from my experience, they're all good people. They have a reputation for manufacturing problems, but I've never seen them create something that wasn't already there. The producers might ask you about

This photo was taken while the show was airing. Thank
goodness Lauren and I found an instant connection
and stayed connected after filming ended.

the drama going on in the house or how you feel. They might
encourage you to do something you ordinarily might not. But
they would never force you to do anything you don't want to. I
never saw a producer do anything malicious or hurtful to get a

good story out of it. It should be common sense to anyone on the show not to tell the producers anything you don't want to be known. At the end of the day they do have a job to do.

I've also heard people say the producers got them drunk and that's why they acted a certain way. Sure, there is usually enough alcohol around to sink a ship, but nobody is forcing anyone to have a drink. Sweet Lace got way too drunk on the first night, and that sloppy impression started her off on the wrong foot. I think about that now when I'm on dates and give myself a one-, maybe two-, drink rule.

Getting tipsy is easy to do during taping because there is so much champagne around. That and your nerves drive you to have a few sips, just to take the edge off. But the hours are long, and it's easy to overdrink. Have you ever noticed that in the first episode of every season the sun is out at the end of the first mixer? That's because they often film that scene through the night, into the morning. Nobody is nursing the same drink that entire time. On top of the alcohol, you're exhausted from the long days and nights that turn into mornings. It's the perfect recipe for drama and overly exaggerated emotions. I reminded myself constantly to slow down and not be the drunk girl, although it didn't always work out. On our first group date, I was definitely drunk. In fact, I was so hammered I cried when I didn't get the rose. Talk about embarrassing! I was pretty mortified watching it later. I mean, I was upset because I wanted that rose . . . but crying? Come on.

Being on *The Bachelor* was like being aboard a tight ship. When it came to shooting, everything was very structured with a precise schedule. We were expected to wake up at a certain time every morning and could only hang out in designated areas. If you're going on a group or one-on-one date, then you're part of the production schedule. But if you're not involved with what is being shot, it's a long day of doing nothing. We'd basically sit around all day waiting to be a part of the show. We'd paint our nails, nap, pretty much just hang. There wasn't a whole lot of freedom. When we were in Las Vegas, our hotel had a gym and sauna, which we were allowed to visit. That was a huge bonus. It was nothing like lounging around the Bachelor mansion. Still, whether dating or doing my nails, I always felt very aware of the cameras because they were right in my face, and there was no forgetting that I was being filmed.

"Traveling" with the show was funny because we spent the majority of the time not traveling or sightseeing at all but secluded from the world, in a hotel room or in the Bachelor mansion. The only people we saw regularly were each other and the producers for what seemed like so long. The only time we saw other people out in public was at the airport when traveling to a new destination. Being such a big group, we stood out, and, since the show hadn't aired yet, nobody knew who we were. Sometimes we were approached at the airport by someone asking, "Are you guys filming *The Bachelor*?!" The producers would throw people off by saying we were en route to a volleyball tournament or cheerleading competition.

We all went crazy at the airport shops because we could finally swipe our cards to buy something. If there was a MAC

Cosmetics or even a duty-free store we would all stock up on makeup and perfume. It was silly how much we missed simple things such as making a purchase. And we took advantage of opportunities to buy things we may have forgotten at home. The packing list provided by the show was pretty broad, so we were supposed to have everything we could possibly need. We were told to bring clothes for all four seasons: snow boots, bikinis, down coats, sandals. We were also told to pack for all occasions: working out, hiking, dancing, and so on. Then, of course, there were the cocktail dresses for each rose ceremony. For shoes, I thought it would be smart to pack two pairs of heels, plain black and basic nude.

Would you believe all of these outfits and accessories, plus hair tools and makeup, all had to fit in just two suitcases? That's right: We were limited to just two suitcases! And imagine having to pack these suitcases before every rose ceremony, because everyone does. Even if you are certain you're getting a rose, you have to pack your bags every three days. I definitely became an expert packer!

Though we visit many exciting destinations, it's anything but a vacation for the cast and crew. When you see us in the Bahamas or Mexico, we don't actually get to leave the hotel room unless we are going on a date. That's right, *the hotel room.* Even the beach, pool, and gym are off limits. So even though we get to travel to these amazing places we don't really get to see much of them. Now when I see *The Bachelor* casts traveling to the Maldives or somewhere halfway around the world, I feel kind of bad for them! Imagine traveling for twenty hours and arriving somewhere only to get sent right back without having even seen the place. Now you might understand why we're so excited to get a date card!

For the most part, the producers pick excellent bachelors (minus a few), and I still think Ben is one of the best. Even though Ben and I didn't have overwhelming chemistry, I really wanted it to work with him because I knew he was the kind of guy who would make my life better. He was kind and forthcoming, and he had the same values I did. All the things I was missing in my previous marriage.

I decided to tell Ben about my daughters on week two. It was so important for me to tell him early on, but deciding when and how was very difficult. I knew it had to be during a one-on-one and not part of a group conversation. I didn't want to wait for the first date, either. Talk about a mood killer. Besides, if Ben was going to ask me out, he needed to know who I really was, and, first and foremost, that was a mother. Walking toward Ben, I was flooded with thoughts: *Could my ex be right about no guy ever wanting me again? Would Ben agree with Olivia's sentiment that I reminded her of a "Teen Mom"?* The answer: not at all. Not only was Ben okay with me being a mom, he was intrigued and wanted to know more about the girls. He even seemed to like me more after I shared this with him. I felt very reassured that I would be okay. Not just there on the show but in general, in real life.

My first date in too many years took place in a hot air balloon floating over Mexico City. It was also the only time I got to leave the hotel room during our stay. Looking back on my big date with Ben, I cringe over how many times I say "like." That's how nervous I was! I was terrified, and it wasn't due to a fear of heights. I'd gotten over the hurdle of telling Ben I was a single mom, but what he didn't know was I had just gotten out of a really bad marriage. Kids are cute and everything, but there was nothing adorable about my last relationship. I was conflicted about opening up regarding my painful past. Did he need to know? How much detail is too much? Up until now Ben had only known me as a carefree and fun girl. I didn't want to scare him with the less-than-sunny details, but I wanted to be honest about what my life was really like. The truth was, I had baggage. Many people break up with an ex and never have to deal with them again, but when there are children involved, the ex is still going to be a part of your life. It was only fair to let Ben in on these details because he was considering being a part of that life.

Introducing Ben to my kids was a huge deal. It was the first time the girls would see me with a man other than their dad. I genuinely thought Ben and I might end up together, so I bent my own rule about introducing a guy so early on. In addition, I felt a little pressured by producers to hit fast forward. I knew this was a scene they really wanted to film and I didn't see any harm in it.

Ben was so sweet and gentle with Kins and Char. He was patient and made them feel special. It made my heart swell. Seeing a guy I was dating gel with the girls so naturally, while being present and attentive, was almost too much to take. I felt like I was seeing a glimpse of what our future could be.

But . . . how can you resist these two little cuties?!

After our date with the girls, I thought there was no way he'd send me home. Why would producers allow me to expose my children to this guy—and, not to mention, to the world—unless they knew I was going to be "the one"? *Surely Ben understood meeting someone's kids is something you only do if you intend on sticking around,* I thought. In hindsight I realize how truly naïve I was back then. At the end of the day producers are there to create content for entertainment, not to look out for my best interest. Since I was the first hometown date before Lauren, JoJo, and Caila, I knew I'd have to wait a week to see or talk to Ben. What I didn't realize was the next time I'd see him would be at the rose ceremony. I thought I'd get a chance to see or talk to him beforehand, but it didn't happen that way. My heart sank when he let me go, but it wasn't because he didn't choose me. I was saddened over the way I was let go. Ben could have come to my hotel before the ceremony to let me know about his choice. That is always an option for the Bachelor. He also could have pulled me aside and given me a heads-up. I didn't expect special treatment, but I'd hoped for extra sensitivity since I had just let him in on the two things that mean the most to me in this world.

Once I got home, I wasn't heartbroken, but I was bummed. It wasn't like the love of my life had just dumped me. In fact, as much as I liked Ben because he has fantastic qualities, we could all see the connection between him and Lauren. At some point we all realized the final rose would belong to Lauren.

Although I have zero regrets, if I went on the show today things would be very different. I've changed so much since being on season twenty. Watching myself on *The Bachelor,* I realize how traumatized I was by my last relationship. My self-esteem was in the toilet, and I was always so nervous and lacking any real confidence. The show found me when I was naïve and unsure of myself. Fortunately, I left the show a better version of me, having learned so much about myself. Believe it or not, being on a reality show gives you a great opportunity to express your feelings—all the time. You are encouraged to openly talk about your insecurities and fears, and, in turn, you learn you're not alone. It is a very emotional experience that cracks you open, leaving you vulnerable and honest.

I found myself talking about things I'd never talk about on a daily basis, things like my past, my family, and how outside influences affect me. Being on the show taught me to be more expressive about how I feel. To this day, when I am in a relationship I communicate my feelings and I ask for the same in return. Before, I would try to guess what others were thinking, but now I realize it's okay to ask questions and share. It feels really good to be open and talk about these things.

The Rose: You're Never Stuck

Finding someone new was the last thing on my mind after getting divorced. I thought constantly of the words my ex said to me: "You can't divorce me. You'll be twenty-five and divorced with two kids. No one will want you." Regardless of whether you were married with kids, got engaged, dated for six weeks, or only had one fantastic date, there's always a sense of, "Oh crap, do I really have to start all over again?" Going on *The Bachelor* as a single mother, I felt certain that Ben would have roses banned from the mansion before handing one to me week after week. But he didn't. In fact, he was totally cool with me having two kids. My ex was 100 percent wrong. (I love saying that.)

The Thorns

- As hard is it can be, try not to compare yourself to other people.
- Don't let your past stand in the way of your future.
- Build up other women around you. Being a girls' girl is the only way to be!
- On dates, dig deeper for more meaningful conversations.

- If you're a single mom, be upfront from the beginning to avoid an awkward situation later.
- When drinking, know your limits. Not only might you make a fool of yourself but you might fool yourself into thinking you like someone more than you do.
- Don't introduce a guy to your kids when he's dating other women.

Chapter Three

What to Do with All That Baggage (The Good Kind, That Is)

WHEN IT CAME TO PACKING for *The Bachelor,* I put a lot of time and thought into every single item that would join me on the journey. There are two things I knew about myself that would be a challenge when it came to the two-suitcase rule: One, I like to have options when I'm traveling and two, I'm really, really bad at minimizing the things I bring—especially clothes. What if I get too hot? Too cold? What if it's too windy? What if I spill something on myself while eating and the stain refuses to leave? It also didn't help knowing that if I forgot something, I couldn't just run to a local store to purchase it as I could in my regular life.

I decided to do some "research" by watching reruns of old seasons of *The Bachelor.* Turns out, that didn't help me much and made me even more doubtful about what to bring. *How do they fit all those rose ceremony gowns into two suitcases, along with everything else?* I wondered, frustrated. I certainly had no idea where we'd be going or the types of activities we'd be doing. Stuck in my angst about cramming everything into two suitcases only, I decided to buckle down and implement some sort of system. In this chapter, I'll share the way I coordinated outfits and packed for the show, along with tips and tricks for how you can do the same for your vacations.

Tip: Take printed or digital photos of every single outfit you're going to wear on your trip. To be sure you don't miss anything, make sure all accessories and details are visible in the photo.

One night, I had my friends, my mom, and my sister come over to help me lay everything out on my living room floor. They gladly did this in exchange for some pizza and wine. It would also be the last time in potentially three months that I would see them, so it was a nice way to decompress from all the anxiety and nervousness from going on the show, too.

Pre-planning each outfit was serious business. My whole closet was torn apart by the time we decided exactly what I was going to bring. We turned my living room into a full-blown fitting room. One by one, I tried on each outfit (the worst part, because I *hate* having to try anything on) to make sure that everything fit properly and was cutely coordinated.

Try It On!

Once, when preparing for a work trip, I got so incredibly lazy that I legitimately threw everything into a suitcase and called it a day. Since it was a highly publicized social media influencer event, I ordered a bunch of super cute clothes online to bring. I was pretty confident in my choices and thought, *I've ordered from this site before. It should be fine.* But guess what? It wasn't fine. Half of the clothes didn't fit me, and I ended up having to improvise different tactics just to stop it from causing a wardrobe malfunction or slipping off me mid-step! I didn't have safety pins either, so I was straight-up using hair ties or rubber bands to tighten and secure things at the waist. I kid you not, I could pinpoint specific pictures on my Instagram where, if you looked closely, you'd see there was some sort of creative alteration on my outfits. Since that trip, I always—*always!*—try things on to ensure they fit well and keep me covered in the right places before putting them anywhere near my suitcase.

Once I tried everything on to make sure it fit well, I then did a round of backup options where I paired the same bottoms with a different top, or vice versa. One thing that you have to understand about the show is that there is a lot, I mean a *lot*, of footage being filmed. Half of the outfits I brought with me didn't even make it on camera. There were moments on the show where I repeated bottoms or tops, but it probably wasn't that noticeable because I didn't get screen time wearing it or they chose to air something different. When it came to repeat options, I made sure that they were staple pieces that could go with multiple tops or bottoms. For example, I packed three different washes of denim jeans (black, dark blue, and light blue) and did the same for my shorts. I also packed a ton of the same style camis but in different colors. Today, I use the same rule when packing for a trip, and I suggest you do the same. Your staple items depend on the weather where you are going, but they generally include denim jeans and/or denim shorts and either basic tees or solid camis to go alone or under something. You can mix and match them with basically everything while dressing them up or down.

Once we narrowed down the "priority" outfits (in case I got kicked off early) and "option twos," we then got even more detailed, labeling each photo with "rose ceremony," "group date," and "date." Needless to say, it was a mission! But the time we spent preparing made my life a million times easier on the show. Again, I use this tactic in my regular travels now. I'll plan by labeling ahead of time what outfits are for nice dinners, daytime activities, business meetings, and so on.

After everyday wear and outfits, we moved on to swimwear. Swimwear is pretty easy because it usually doesn't take up too much space, but the hard part about swimwear is the accessories that you'll bring to go with it. You may have noticed on social media that I'm never without statement or dangly earrings when I'm wearing a swimsuit or bikini. I don't usually like loud prints, so I always go for solids. Keep in mind, solid colors can always pair with other solid colors, so if you're having trouble finding space in your luggage, ditch any printed swimwear and only bring colors that you can mix and match together.

Tip: Remember that simple clothing choices can always be elevated or feel more styled with accessories. Often a white t-shirt, denim jeans, and a layer of dainty necklaces and bracelets does the trick.

Hats, mini neck scarves, dainty jewelry, and a good pair of shoes are what I feel take my outfits to the next level. If you're running low on space, pack just the basics when it comes to clothes but pile on the accessories.

At the end of the night, we were pizza-less and two wine bottles down, but that was the least of our worries. I had all the perfect outfits, but how was I going to basically get 75 percent of my closet into two suitcases, and, on top of that, all my hair products, makeup, skincare, and shoes? I also couldn't forget my pajamas, workout clothes, and some hair extensions (just being real with you guys!).

Here are the best solutions I've found when it comes to fitting as many things as possible into suitcases:

1. Rolling clothes instead of folding them. This is such a small and simple change, but it makes a huge difference. I can fit nearly twice as many shirts into a suitcase when I roll my clothes.

I think I need to reread this chapter and take some of my
own advice. This was for a three-day trip. Don't do what I did
since I didn't even wear 90 percent of what I packed!

2. Packing cubes. I don't know where my life would be without packing cubes. They don't even need to be fancy ones! I get many of mine from Amazon.com, in all different prints, shapes, and sizes. I always roll my clothes into packing

cubes, and it's just so much more organized. What I also like about packing cubes is that nothing moves around when your suitcase is being transported from location to location.

3. Vacuum-sealed bags for clothes. This is kind of an aggressive way of packing, and I didn't do this for the show, but I really wish I had. It is so affordable and easily available on Amazon.com, and I bet it would have saved me so much time when it came to stuffing everything into my luggage.

4. A travel jewelry case. A travel jewelry organizer is the one thing I never knew I needed. It keeps all my necklaces untangled and all my rings organized in one location. All the statement earrings I bring on trips fit perfectly beneath the top layer that usually holds all the rings and keeps them from getting damaged or lost.

Leading up to the show, so many thoughts and questions popped into my head. I thought a lot about how Ben would be in person, but honestly, most of my thoughts were consumed by the other girls. These women were the ones I'd be living with, traveling with, and getting to know on a daily basis. On top of that, we'd be secured in a mansion with no cell phones or knowledge of the outside world. I just remember praying for one good friend from whom I could steal toothpaste if I happened to run out. Thank goodness, on my season we had an amazing group of girls who shared anything and everything.

There were a couple of times when someone had a fashion emergency and a lot of creative thinking came into play. If you're going on a trip that's anything like a *Bachelor* excursion (sans producers, cameras, and that whole multiple-women-fighting-for-the-attention-of-one-man thing), you'll want to avoid having to use bandages as pasties or rubber bands as safety pins. These fashion emergencies can happen on any excursion, whether it's your friend's destination wedding or your partner's company gala. I recommend stocking up on:

- Pasties. And a lot of them. I would pack some reusable ones, so you can salvage them, and some that are meant for one-time use. You never know when someone might need you to save the day, and you'd be able to give her a fresh pair instead of the ones you wore the night before.
- NUDE undergarments. Everything nude! Nude is the holy grail color for bras and panties and will always match well with everything and anything. Bring more than a couple of thongs, but if you're not someone who likes thongs, I definitely recommend nude, seamless underwear, seamless being the key word. Bodycon and hip-hugging underwear do not make for a good combination—not on national television, not anywhere.
- Simple nude heels. And the same exact pair in black. Nude and black are two staple colors that will go with anything in your wardrobe. If you needed a last-minute spruce-up to your outfit, throwing on a heel could change everything. Lots of times, I panicked because I thought maybe I wouldn't be dressed up enough. No one ever really discloses the location of where you're going, so it's important to be prepared for all sorts of situations.

Being with the girls in the house was one of my favorite things about being on *The Bachelor*. We spent so much time together, and it really was like a flashback to college in a giant sorority house with lots and lots of food and drinks. We'd laugh together, share our frustrations, cry, eat, and drink. We'd get ready together, clip in each other's hair extensions, dye each other's roots, pluck each other's brows (Lauren B's Brow Bar came in handy real fast), and give each other manicures and pedicures. We did anything that would pass the time, whether it was playing weird games with food or trying to motivate each other to work out.

Thinking back, I almost didn't pack any workout gear, because I thought maybe because I couldn't really go to a traditional gym or take a cycling class, I wouldn't need to bring my workout shoes. I really just wanted to believe that I didn't need to pack my tennis shoes because they took up a lot of space, and also because I would find any reason I could not to exercise! Having no shoes would be a great one. I was so grateful that I ended up packing more than one gym outfit because working out was and is a great way for me to clear my mind. It helped with my anxiety, especially the worry I felt being away from my girls for so long. Now, when I go on a trip, I always pack a pair of tennis shoes and at least a few outfits to train in. Even if it's just a power walk around the property or a run around a resort, I always feel so much better about myself afterward.

Again, suitcase space when it came to packing for *The Bachelor* was so precious that I decided just to pack one pair of black yoga leggings and two dark-colored sports bras so that they wouldn't get dirty too quickly. My black leggings ended up being great loungewear during downtime around the house, a bonus being they matched with everything I brought.

Because we didn't pack any weights (of course), I often used wine bottles (lots of those lying around) and my own body weight for running through different circuits. I now wish I'd studied more equipment-free workout guides before getting to the mansion and packed resistance bands, booty bands, or even a jump rope. Even if you don't have a mansion as your destination, I recommend the same! These items don't take up much space and would make it easier for you to get an effective workout in when the gym isn't an option.

Thanks to *The Bachelor*, packing workout gear and equipment is something I always do now, and I will always call the hotel where I'm staying to double-check if it has a decent gym or any studio classes I would be interested in. Regardless, I stick to the same formula when it comes to bringing gym clothes for traveling: black yoga pants or leggings, a dark-colored sports bra, and some easy-to-pack gym equipment.

Tip: Keep your workout gear fresh by layering dryer sheets between your gym clothes when packing. It's an impromptu way of having your clothes smell like they were freshly washed.

A big question I asked myself before even going on the show was how the girls managed to maintain everything—and by everything, I mean *everything.* Typically, bikini waxes are every four to five weeks, gel manicures are every two to three weeks, eyebrow maintenance is every two to three weeks, and eyelash extensions are every two weeks too! Granted, you can prolong certain treatments if you maintain it well (like tweezing straggling eyebrow hairs), but you could really only keep everything under control for so long. I was nervous about packing enough skincare and hair care too, and had heard conflicting reports about the producers being able to provide you with certain beauty products. To avoid running out of anything I needed, I had to be really careful about the number of products I brought. Fortunately, there were many girls who had each other's backs, so I was never lacking any product.

I learned quickly that being in a house full of girls meant that it was like a sampling bar at Sephora. We shared so much makeup and tips and tricks from each other, it was actually really fun. When it came to packing all of my beauty products for the trip, I ended up getting two giant vanity bags that kept everything organized. I kept my brushes in one area, eye shadows in another zipped compartment, and lip stains in another. I made sure to stock up on makeup wipes (which were long gone by the end of my trip). Before the trip, I kept the same makeup organizers for years before switching to other ones. I never wanted to splurge on vanity organizers, figuring I could just stuff everything into smaller makeup bags or pouches. But I learned it's helpful to have your beauty items very organized because you end up spending less time getting ready, meaning more time enjoying yourself. Plus, when you're in a mansion with girls who also have lots of makeup, it's good to keep yours organized in one area. It's also a guarantee that nothing will spill onto the rest of your luggage if it's damaged during transit or if your eyeshadow palettes crack.

While on the subject of beauty, I often get questions about how I do my makeup when I'm traveling. I prefer to be makeup free most of the time when I'm in humid weather, but I had to figure out certain types of products that work for my skin based on guesses of where we would be going. Of course, *The Bachelor* mansion is in Los Angeles, so there's already an indication that the weather would be warm. One of my hero products on any trip, though, is a makeup-setting spray. I have been using Urban Decay's All Nighter spray for *years*, and it's something that I've recommended over and over again. While that setting spray is my favorite, I know that it doesn't work for everyone's skin, but, hands down, a setting spray is absolutely necessary. That, plus waterproof eyeliner and mascara. There are two things guaranteed when you're on *The Bachelor*: Either you're going to be shedding some tears or you're going to be in a pool or the ocean. I made it a huge point to bring the right type of makeup that I knew would outlast any traumatizing situation. While I hope you won't be shedding any tears on your future trips, you want to be prepared to battle an impromptu jump into the sea or unexpected splash from the pool.

Packing can be a nightmare in any circumstance, but it was especially difficult for *The Bachelor* because there were so many uncertainties. I never knew what locations we'd be in, and none of us really knew how long we were going to be on the show. Luckily, in the real world chances are you'll have a better handle on what the day will bring. Hopefully these tips will shed some light on how best to prepare for your journey, wherever it takes you!

I'm so grateful for the cool places I've been. This is one of the most unique places I've traveled to, in Morocco!

Chapter Four

Bachelor's Degree in Dating

WHEN I RETURNED HOME from filming *The Bachelor* I felt empowered. Not only did I begin to believe I would get a second chance at finding love, I knew I deserved a good guy like Ben who wouldn't go behind my back or abandon me and the girls. I was excited to put myself back out there. Going on the show was sort of like taking a crash course in dating. The lessons I learned over two short months of filming were ones that might have taken me years to otherwise experience. This education served me well as I applied the advice I gathered from my unreal life to my real one—and now I'm sharing these top tips with you.

Date Yourself

While I was on a boy break and busy just being a mom, daughter, and friend, I learned a lot about myself. In retrospect, it was a blessing in disguise. I got to rediscover who I was. No matter how independent you are, you lose a little bit of yourself in a relationship. Post-breakup, we're presented with an opportunity to be our most authentic selves, and that's a pretty cool thing. Learning how to be okay on my own and be happy with myself was something I had to achieve before even entertaining the thought of finding a partner. In my experience, the worst time to start dating is when we're lonely or sad because, when we do so, we end up settling for less than what we want and deserve.

Show Your Single Self Some Love

After my divorce, I was a stressed-out momma, always overcome with worry and anxiety. I never took time to make myself feel good. Whether you're a mom or not, it's essential to treat yourself every now and then by getting your nails done, fitting in a blowout, relaxing with a massage, or even taking a long walk or hike. You just have to make the time. When we were filming season twenty, little moments like having the twins do my makeup made me feel so great! I remember thinking that when I got home I needed to make feeling pretty and rejuvenated more of a priority.

Take Time to Appreciate

Even though I was worried about being sent home on a daily basis, I was able to focus on the great friendships I made on the show. Filming wasn't stressful for me on any level because the silver lining was so strong. One thing I regret as a mom is when Kins and Char were babies I was so upset about our situation I can't really remember the good times as well. I think my brain

Taking small trips with the girls and having fun moments really kept me optimistic through a painful time in my life.

blocked out the period of time when I was so overcome by my messy divorce, and unfortunately that time includes precious moments with my babies. I wish I'd been able to say to myself, "This is very hard and divorce is awful, but you're healthy and you have your healthy, happy kids. Life is still good." These days, rather than focusing on what isn't working, I've learned to focus on what *is*. It's difficult in the moment, but like any practice it gets better the more you do it. Trust me, appreciation for what you do have helps you get through the rougher days.

Be the Bachelorette

Just because you don't have cameras following you around the clock doesn't mean you shouldn't apply the same elimination standards used on the show. After dating around a bit, we have at least a general idea of what we do and don't want. On the show, you're hoping to be chosen, but in real life, oh no, honey. Don't wait to be chosen—be the chooser. Remember that you are the prize, and it's not only okay but absolutely necessary to be picky even from the start.

For example, if you catch him lying, no rose. Does he look you in the eye when you're having a conversation? Rose. Does he show compassion when someone's in a tough spot? Rose. Does he have a hard time taking responsibility or apologizing when he's in the wrong? No rose. The same goes for digital dating. If he's photographed with a different girl in every picture, I'm swiping left. If he's got a few family photos in there,

I'm swiping right. Remember the red flags of your past and use them to guide you toward a happier future!

He's Dating Other Girls, and That's Okay

On *The Bachelor*, it's no secret that the guy you're dating is seeing other girls. In real life, until you've had "the talk," everything, and everyone, is fair game. It's easy to put yourself in a pretend relationship before things become official, but that's the way of the girls who fall by the wayside—fast. On my season of *The Bachelor*, both Olivia and Lace considered Ben to be their boyfriend from the first day of filming. Olivia was very vocal with us girls about how she was the only one for Ben. She would constantly throw jabs my way by saying Ben wasn't ready to raise someone else's kids. Lace would act out in wild ways every time Ben turned his attention to another girl. She'd steal conversations, sob hysterically, and act . . . well, kinda crazy. The possessive behavior these girls exhibited ended up costing them each a rose. While filming, I discovered a healthy mind-set that kept me sane and still in the game. You've got to keep your cool while things are still heating up. If he's dating other girls, I say keep dating other guys.

Why So Serious?

Many people compare dating to a full-time job. I sure hope they love what they do! Meeting new people and exploring your city should be exciting and fun. Whenever I feel bummed about a lackluster date or an unreturned text, I think about the twins, Hayley and Emily. It's not just for show—these sisters are always having a great time. The twins are able to see the fun and find happiness in every situation. Even when they shed a tear, it's followed by a smile. They support each other and others, plus they are unapologetically themselves at all times. I admire how these girls are able to uplift themselves and put a sunny perspective on basically any situation.

Empty Baggage

I was extremely nervous to open up to Ben about my previous marriage. My hesitation came from a fear that he'd be scared away or view it as a big red flag. I think most divorced women and single moms are worried we'll be seen as damaged goods because we have been there, done that, and it didn't work. Watching the other girls' dates, I realized everyone has some form of baggage. We all have insecurities and a past.

For me, being honest right off the bat is always the best way. I learned it's best to work my kids into the conversation early on so my date doesn't feel misled and also so I don't feel like I'm concealing my truth. Does he need to know every detail of my divorce? No way. Should I carry on about my custody drama? Nope. When it comes to dating, I believe we should be honest but focus on where we are going as opposed to where we have been.

The Villain Never Wins

It would be very mean-girl of me to call out the mean girls on the show. Chances are you've known a mean girl or two in your life or perhaps have been one yourself (we've all had our moments). The thing is, there's nothing good that can come from conniving or sabotaging others' happiness. My on-show and real-life persona is that of a good girl—and trust me when I say that's who I am to the core. But, for the sake of honesty, I'll admit that it's not always easy taking the high road. I've been very tempted to be the villain and go against my good-girl instincts. Sure, I've wanted to bad-mouth others by airing my hurt feelings over social media, but really, who would that hurt in the end? Me (and my kids). As impossible as it seems in the moment, it is far easier to cease fire when someone is spreading rumors or throwing shade your way. During a very public breakup, one of my ex-boyfriends did a lot of talking to the media. I did a lot of trash talking too—to my close friends and family. But when it came to the media I did my best to keep what I put out there classy. In the end, it felt incredible to maintain my dignity and show my girls what resilience, strength, and a true good girl look like.

Be Like Lauren

One of the best parts of being on *The Bachelor* was meeting my best friend, Lauren Bushnell. She might have walked away with the final rose, but I like to think I'm the real winner. I knew immediately that Lauren was a special person. She is a real girls' girl and has an honest, authentic, laid-back vibe. Watching our season after the fact, I had a huge *aha!* moment. When Ben asked Lauren if she'd be devastated should she not receive a rose at the upcoming ceremony, Lauren told him without hesitation that she'd be okay if she didn't get it. Like many viewers, I thought, "She's toast." Yet, if you watch this scene closely, you'll notice Ben's eyes light up. I believe it was in this moment that Ben became further mystified by this cool and confident woman. Lauren's answer was clear: She wanted him, but she didn't need him. This is a fantastic lesson to us all. We each *want* someone to be our partner in life, but, if the last five years have taught me anything, it's that we don't *need* them to complete us.

One thing I've learned is that relationships are hard work. But sometimes no matter how much you're willing to work on things, it's just not meant to be. I tend to put my entire heart into my relationships. I go all in, which makes it really hard to end things. I'm not one of those people who can easily walk away from things I know aren't right for me. There are so many reasons why I find it's hard for me to quit, but one of them is definitely because getting back into the dating world scares the heck out of me. When I start to lose hope and see one of my relationships crumbling, I'd be lying if I said that the questions "Am I ever going to find someone?" or "How do I even start

So grateful to be surrounded by women like Lauren who can be honest about relationships and who I can turn to for advice.

dating . . . again?!" don't cross my mind. I mean, how do you meet someone organically these days?

When I first went on *The Bachelor*, dating apps like Tinder and Bumble were fairly new. I swore to myself I would never use any form of online dating. I had some friends who said it worked for them, but I figured it wasn't for me. I just knew I was destined to meet someone in the produce section at Whole Foods, in line at Starbucks, or at a friend's wedding. Honestly, I would have been cool with meeting someone at a bar! Just not online. The whole thing felt so . . . unromantic.

After I came home from the show, about five months went by without me going on a single date. I didn't mind—it felt so good to be taking time for myself and the girls without any guy drama to spoil it. I was slowly gaining the confidence back that had been completely ruined in my last relationship. When I finally was feeling happy, independent, and whole, I realized I was ready to start dating again.

But no matter how dolled up I got to go grocery shopping I never seemed to run into the love of my life. The reality started to set in that meeting someone at Whole Foods or Starbucks, or even at a bar jam-packed with mingling singles, isn't quite as common as it appeared in my favorite rom-coms. My single friends seemed to be going on dates and texting with new guys, but I wasn't having any luck. *So, how do you meet people these days?* I wondered. Finally, I decided to give online dating a chance. Turns out dating apps aren't as crazy as I once thought. Ninety percent of the guys my friends were going on dates with or talking to they met on dating apps. After listening to some good, bad, and funny dating app stories, I thought at the very least it would be worth a few fun stories of my own. Even though a big part of me still feels—to this day—that meeting someone online is artificial and unromantic since you're judging people based on a few photos, I figured it was worth a shot.

During a girls' night out, my friends Lauren Bushnell and Caila Quinn convinced me to download the Bumble app. They helped me create a profile, which consists of choosing the perfect photos (see "Choosing Photos for Your Profile" sidebar) and bio (ditto) and helped me start swiping. I was having fun with it and not taking it at all too seriously. We were laughing at some of the profiles because they can be so ridiculous. I've never seen so many guys flexing their abs for mirror selfies in my life. SWIPE LEFT. It was a big mistake handing Lauren my phone because she swiped right on a few too many guys. I'd say we swiped more than 300 profiles that night. Of those, there were maybe three guys I swiped right on that I actually

Choosing Photos for Your Profile

1. Make sure to use a variety of photos that show who you are as a person. Don't just choose the six photos you think you look the best in. You need to show your personality! Include places you've traveled, hobbies you enjoy, activities you participate in. This also gives the other person a topic to touch on when they reach out to you.

2. If you're a single parent like me, I encourage you to include at least one photo with your kids. If you aren't comfortable with that, mention that you have kids in your bio. You don't want to waste time talking to or dating someone only to

find out they're not cool with you being a parent. Let them know right off the bat! If you match, you already know they're cool with your situation.

3. Related to the previous point, if you're not a parent, consider skipping photos of you with babies and kids. To me, it looks a little desperate, like you're trying to prove something: "Look, kids like me! I'm going to make a great parent!" Also, as a single mom it really bothers me when guys post a picture with a baby or kid and then comment, "Don't worry, the kid's not mine!" To be real, I find that insulting, because it adds to the stigma that there's something undesirable about being a single parent.

4. Make sure you look like your photos! Don't post multiple photos of you with sunglasses on, heavily Photoshopped pictures, or anything from too many years ago. It's important to be transparent. If you're planning to eventually meet that person, you want them to recognize you.

5. Include your Instagram handle. Once again, do so only if you're comfortable with it. If someone can do their research on you and get more insight into your life and personality, the chances are you'll have a better first date. And vice versa. It's hard to judge someone based on a couple of photos and a paragraph bio.

6. Make sure your main photo is one of just YOU. The last thing you want is a guy you think is cute swiping in hopes that you're actually your BFF. It's okay to post group photos and photos with friends. I actually encourage it. But just make sure your main photo is a solo shot!

would have gone on a date with. But I guess that's what makes it a numbers game.

One of those guys was a really handsome soccer player. The next day, I was so excited when I got a notification that we matched! On Bumble, girls have to message the guys first. I don't necessarily like this concept. I prefer a guy to pursue me. But that's the name of the game in this case, so I was in. Of course, I started a group chat with my friends and asked, "What do I say? How long do I wait to message him?" The best I could come up with was, "Hey, I'm Amanda!"

LAME. I know. My advice would be to *not* start a conversation that way. Now I know the best tactic is to ask the other person a question about him or her. Or at the very least ask how their day is going. But, at the time, I was nervous and dating via apps was new to me! And I thought it was enough to start the conversation if he really was interested. We ended up exchanging numbers and texting for a few days, and then he asked me to grab a coffee a few days later. It went really well for a first date. He was cuter in person (I found most guys are!) and very sweet, and we had a lot in common. I was leaving for a trip the next day, and we agreed to go on a second date when I got back in town.

I'm a girl who lives by her word, so I thought it was strange when weeks went by and I hadn't heard from him. The dating term used for this is called "ghosting." He ghosted me. Never talked to me again! After digging a little deeper on his Instagram page, as any modern girl in the dating world would do, I found out he had a girlfriend. So, for my first dating app experience, I got ghosted by a guy with a girlfriend! Go figure. I'm assuming from my detective work that they broke up, he went on Bumble and went on some dates, and then they got back together. Perhaps I dodged a bullet. And who knows, maybe they're living happily ever after, which, you know, good for them.

It turns out that guys with girlfriends or even married men will go on dating apps. Shocker, I know! For that reason, my number one rule for using dating apps is to do your research before going on a date. Get their last name and stalk their Instagram pages! There's no shame in background checking. Know what you're getting into. Some people will even include their Instagram handle in their dating app profiles, making it super easy to investigate. Look at their social media pages and get more of an idea of who that person is or at least what they're all about. Maybe you'll discover more of their hobbies or that you have mutual friends . . . but hopefully you don't discover that they're already in a relationship!

I went on a couple more Bumble first dates. None of them turned into second dates. But still, I was enjoying myself. One thing I learned from dating apps is that dating doesn't have to be a serious husband search—it can actually be fun! I tried out a couple other apps as well, and I learned to enjoy the journey of meeting new people while keeping an open mind and heart.

Chapter Five

Good Talk

WITH EVERYTHING I LEARNED from being on *The Bachelor*, it took me only one trip to paradise to abandon it all. We all make mistakes, and this was my big one. If my newly found self-esteem and empowerment could be compared to sobriety, let's just say I fell off the wagon. Hard.

In the months following *The Bachelor*, I was casually seeing a really nice guy I met on a dating app. He was patient and sweet, humble and easygoing. We didn't have much chemistry, but I was trying to give him a chance because I knew he was a really good guy. We never made it to official boyfriend–girlfriend status, yet when *Bachelor in Paradise* came calling, I was still very hesitant to sign on. I wasn't sure it was the right environment for me. The show features former *Bachelor* and *Bachelorette* cast members who travel to a secluded beach resort in Mexico. Everyone is single and looking to connect with someone, and those who don't find a fling are sent home. The show is racier and much more sexually charged than *The Bachelor*. To me it seemed to be more about hooking up and less about finding "the one." I pictured kids teasing my daughters on the playground, saying, "Ew, your mom was on *Bachelor in Paradise*!"

One month before filming started, I decided that I could participate by acting in a way of which I would be proud. I was still single, after all, and what if I was missing a big opportunity?

Being on *Paradise* is wildly different than being on *The Bachelor*. While *The Bachelor* is very structured and time-constrained, *Paradise* gives you freedom in all aspects. It is almost like being on an actual vacation. You can wake up whenever you like on most days. Producers will put a mic on you, and then you're free to do whatever you want. You can go to the pool, hang at the beach, lounge wherever you feel like it. There aren't many big cameras on you at all times like there are for *The Bachelor*. The cameras are nearby and many are hidden—they're just not so in your face. The only time you have to be aware you're filming is when you go into the water because the microphone packs are not waterproof. If you wanted to go swimming, you had to remove your mic. If you accidentally jumped in the pool with your mic on, the producers would get pretty upset. It happens! Jasmine jumped in the pool with her mic on so many times it became a running joke. Some people thought the ocean might be a safe spot to have a private conversation, but the crew is very aware of all the tricks. As soon as they see two people out in the waves, they get their longest microphones and stick them out as far as they can get them. There really is no way to have a private moment on the show, but again, that's kind of the point. Even with having more time and freedom on *Paradise*, without being able to have a real conversation off camera, how well can you really get to know a person?

Going into *Paradise*, I thought I'd end up dating Nick. We had been flirtatious before when we saw each other out at parties and events pre-*Paradise*, and I liked what I knew of him. So, it was such a bummer when we got to *Paradise* and I had my time alone with Nick, because the chemistry just wasn't there. There were no sparks during my date with Nick, yet viewers were led to believe we were dancing on cloud nine. The truth is, the first and only date Nick and I went on was really awkward. The conversation just didn't flow the way it did when we were around other people. He could hardly hold eye contact with me. Dates can be nerve-racking, but it was strange to me considering the great chemistry we'd had when we had hung out before. I'm still not sure what happened.

After dinner that night, the producers had us try tribal dancing around a fire while playing instruments. We hardly knew each other, so we weren't comfortable doing something so far outside our comfort zone. At that point, we both just wanted the date to be over. Nick was trying his best to be a good sport by playing it up for the cameras but when it was just us, he got quiet. The detached vibes he was giving off showed me he was just not as into it as I hoped we both would be. Later we were sitting by a fire and I could tell the producers were waiting for us to kiss, but the moment just didn't feel right. Nick was asking me questions like "What's your favorite color?" or "What are your favorite pizza toppings?" It couldn't have been less romantic. But I knew the producers weren't going to let the date end until we kissed, so it ended up happening. The kiss wasn't so bad. Actually, it was probably the best part of the date. The date was so cringe-worthy the scenes we shot never even aired. Instead, clever editing made it appear as if Nick and I had a successful first date with a promising future. Not so much.

I'd heard rumors Josh Murray would be showing up to Paradise. I didn't know anything about him other than he was easy on the eyes. Nick and Josh were the last two guys standing during Andi Dorfman's season of *The Bachelorette* and, as we know, she picked Josh. The guys seemingly had a rivalry on and off the show. Josh arrived in Mexico on the heels of my date with Nick. He sat down with a handful of the girls before setting his sights on me. Part of me wonders if his initial attraction to me was influenced by the fact that I had just been on a date with Nick. If another girl had been out with Nick, would she have been in my place?

When I got to watch the show and see how Josh acted after our date, I was appalled. To me he acted sensitive toward the fact I'd just been out with Nick, but when the two were left alone, Josh was so obnoxious and pompous. Josh said in his interview, "There's lions and there's sheep . . . rawr." I suppose that made me the prey? Gross.

Still, Josh got me to fall hard and fast because he said all the right things. It was as if he studied a book on what to say to get me to swoon. I ate it up. Based on what he was telling me, he was spot-on the perfect guy. He loved going to church and volunteering. He claimed to be an empathic guy who loved everyone. He said he couldn't wait for us to be together outside of the show so he could watch the girls while I got manicures with my friends. I thought that was so sweet and cute. *Where has this perfect guy been?* I wondered. Plus, he was already planning a move to California, which I took as a sign that we were meant to be.

Meanwhile, the cast was whispering warnings to me about Josh's dark side. They told me about the book Bachelorette Andi Dorfman had written, much of it having to do with how controlling and cruel Josh was. They told me Josh wasn't as nice and friendly toward them as he was when I was around. When asked about it, Josh fiercely defended himself against Andi's claims. I believed him when he said she was just a bitter ex looking for attention. My head was so far up in the clouds I didn't even consider it a bad sign that an ex-girlfriend was so upset with him she felt compelled to write a book about it.

To be honest, I wasn't completely blinded by the red flags. I began to see signs of bad behavior right away, but I shushed my inner voice and swept anything I didn't want to see under the rug. Even though Josh claimed to be everyone's friend, he didn't really get along with anyone else. On the show you'll see the cast get into little tiffs here and there, but once it's done, it's done. We all get over it and move on fairly quickly. We are like a family in that way. But Josh wouldn't get over those tiffs. He held on to grudges and stayed angry over every little thing.

The level of anger he would have for these small dust-ups was definitely concerning to me, but I figured it was escalated by the environment we were in, not who he really was.

When Nick and Josh got into a fight on the beach, Josh and I discussed leaving. Who needs all this drama? Why are we even here? We already found each other, and we know we want to be together. Why not? The producers immediately intervened. They convinced us to stay by promising the next day we'd have a date card and an overnight in the hotel. One thing about the resort we film at is how hot and sticky it is, with bugs everywhere. Plus we are all sharing same-sex rooms with everyone else on the show so it gets a little crammed. Suffice to say between the bugs and the friends there is very little personal space. The promise of a nice, private room with air conditioning won us back. The producers were good on their word, giving us the date card and an extra night in the fantasy suite, something that never made it to air.

Another thing the public never got to see was Josh's mom, who visited us at our fantasy suite. Awkward? You bet. You want to be ready to meet your boyfriend's family, not meet them unexpectedly from the bed of your fantasy suite. It turned out Josh planned this with the producers and nobody thought to clue me in. Apparently, he felt he couldn't propose unless he could see how I interacted with his mom, so he begged producers to fly her out. I appreciated the sentiment, but still, a heads-up would have been nice. At the time I was in shorts and a cropped top. Not exactly what I would ordinarily wear to meet the parents.

Shortly after Josh left me in the fantasy suite, there was a knock at the door. When I opened it, I was surprised to find Josh and his mom before me. The fact we were all meeting at the fantasy suite, an intimate location where he and I just spent the night together, felt more than just a little inappropriate. The three of us sat on the couch—with cameras rolling, of course—and talked for a long while about my relationship with Josh. His mom didn't take long to mention Andi Dorfman's book, which she had read. She was very concerned about her son after everything he'd gone through following the book's release.

I was surprised by how much his mom wanted to talk about Andi and her book. She asked me how I felt about Josh being so close to his mother and I was honest when I said I found it endearing, being someone who is also close to my parents. She brought it back to Andi, telling me Andi thought the relationship between Josh and his mother was weirdly close. (At first I didn't understand why Andi would feel this way, but further along into our relationship I realized where Andi was coming from.) Josh's mom mentioned she was being overprotective of her son, not wanting him to experience another heartbreak. She advised us to take our time and not rush into anything. It was a pretty serious conversation to be blindsided with, the type of talk for which I would have wanted to be prepared.

When the show began to air and Josh wasn't making a favorable impression on viewers, his mom got worried because she didn't want to look bad in her TV appearance. She demanded approval of the footage before it aired. I saw it and thought it looked like a sweet scene, just us girls talking. But she took too long getting it back to the editors, so ultimately it never aired.

One incident that should have ended things between me and Josh occurred late at night during filming. Everyone was partying, and I was feeling really tired. I told Nick and Jen, who were dating, that they could have the Tree House room. On *Paradise*, there are separate sleeping quarters for the men and the women. There are two rooms where people could sleep together as a couple. After I'd gone to bed in the room I shared with the other girls, Josh caught Nick and Jen as they started walking toward the couples' room. He interjected by insisting, "Amanda and I are staying in there tonight." Nick and Jen explained I told them otherwise.

Instead of being like, "Oh, okay, that's weird; I'll go ask her about it," Josh flew into my room like a psycho, jolted me awake, and yelled at me. I was sort of frozen in bed, not knowing what to do. He cut our conversation short by quipping, "Good talk," and slapped me on the back. I lay in bed that night for hours thinking, *Wow, his anger issues are really bad*. I wondered if his back slap would make it to air. I can't explain why I stayed with Josh after that night. I guess I wanted to believe the stress of the show was getting to him and how he was acting wasn't really who he was. He was, after all, constantly telling me that he's such a good guy. At the time I didn't recognize I was falling into old habits, wanting to protect and defend a broken bird.

I had a pretty good feeling Josh was going to propose on the season finale. I was hopeful things would get better between us because it felt so good to be with someone. It felt so good to be loved. People might assume the producers are really pushing for people to get engaged for the sake of the show, and I'm sure in some cases that's true. In my case, nobody was encouraging me to say yes. If anything, the producers were telling me not to. They'd ask me if I was sure this was something I wanted to do. I was aware they didn't necessarily think Josh was this great guy. In that moment, I felt they were putting my best interest before that of the show. Obviously getting engaged would be great for ratings, but what would it mean for my future?

Once the show started airing, Josh was really excited to see how it all played out, and I thought to myself, *You're going to look really bad, buddy.* And he did. He didn't just look bad to the public. He started to look bad to me. Watching our experience together as an outsider I did see all the red flags, loud and clear. When the slap on the back aired, he claimed it was shifty editing to make him look bad. He wanted me to defend him by publicly blaming production for editing the show to vilify him. But I wouldn't do it. I wasn't about to lie, not even for my fiancé.

Immediately after leaving *Paradise*, Josh and I had our first big argument. He told me on our first date he was planning a move to California, but that story changed the second we stopped filming. He wanted me and the girls to move to

Atlanta. He said Georgia was his home, and he didn't intend to leave it. This was news to me. I would never uproot Kins and Char from their home, and besides, Orange County is where their father lives. It was out of the question.

At the time of this argument, I was committed to attend a charity event in Lake Tahoe along with Ashley Iaconetti, Becca Tilley, and Haley and Emily Ferguson. This event was planned before I even went on *Paradise*, way before Josh came into the picture. Yet Josh tried to convince me not to go, even though he was in Atlanta and I was in Orange County. I explained that my conscience could never let me back out of a charity event. Besides, I *wanted* to go.

Behind my back, Josh started texting the charity organizer and attempting to change my flights. He was supposed to drive from Atlanta to move in with me the following week, but he had such a problem with me going to this charity event that he decided he'd come a week early, in an attempt to get me not to go. For someone who says volunteering is so important to him, his lack of concern for my obligation to this charity didn't seem very charitable to me. For someone who claims not to be controlling, well, I beg to differ. Ashley, Becca, Haley, and Emily could hear him screaming at me on the phone when we were in the car on the way to Tahoe, and they couldn't believe what they heard. I was so embarrassed and confused. I felt like he tricked me into thinking he was a nice, easygoing guy. He was so defensive toward everything Andi claimed he was in her book, but here he was acting exactly like she claimed he did. All this drama came avalanching over me just two weeks post-*Paradise*.

When I returned home, Josh was officially living with me and the girls. It took me all of a day to learn the Lake Tahoe incident was only the beginning. Josh didn't want a fiancée, he wanted a robot he could program and control. After all his sweet talk about wanting to watch the girls while I got manicures with my friends, the reality was he didn't even like me texting or talking to anyone, let alone seeing them in person. One time I met two girls, friends of mine since first grade, for dinner. Josh was so jealous and furious he bombarded me with texts to say he was packing his things and leaving. My attention had to be on Josh and only Josh at all times. I'd have to call my mom from the gym to avoid an issue. I couldn't even listen to male recording artists, especially Justin Bieber! Josh genuinely thought I had an actual crush on the Biebs and taunted me for it, saying I should be embarrassed because I'm a mother. For the record, I don't have a crush on Justin, but I do love his music. For someone who had nothing to hide, I constantly felt like I had to hide everything.

The most bizarre situation that happened during our short engagement would have to be when I caught him spying on me in the shower. I heard him call out through the door, "Are you on the phone?" and I replied, "No! I'm in the shower. Why?"

"I thought I saw you step out," he said.

I glanced down to the floor and saw his head peeping through the bottom crack of the door. I knew then his extreme control issues were far beyond anything I could or wanted to deal with.

The fight that put a nail in the coffin of our relationship happened right after a concert called Jingle Ball a couple of weeks before Christmas. We were hanging out with other *Bachelor* alums, including Ashley. I casually mentioned in conversation with Josh how she and I had had drinks in Lake Tahoe during the charity event. First, let me point out I do not have a drinking problem. Alcohol has never been an issue for me, since I hardly even drink to begin with. Second, in no way did I try to hide the fact we had a few drinks in Lake Tahoe. In fact, I'd posted a picture of me with Haley and Ashley, and I was holding a beer in it. Anyway, Josh completely freaked out. Apparently according to Josh's rules, I wasn't allowed to have a drink with friends on a girls' trip. He completely lost his cool and went crazy, saying some of the meanest things anyone has ever said to me. He even went as far as calling me an awful word. Let's just say it rhymes with "runt."

After he left me at the concert, I told him to sleep at a hotel. For the first time I was actually scared of him, but I'd already stopped believing in us for some time. I realized that there was no reasoning with him and that he would never take responsibility for being in the wrong. I couldn't take the fighting and the distrust. I didn't feel safe or free to be myself, not even in my own home. The next day I let him know we were over, and he needed to move his things out of my house.

I told a few of my friends it was definitely over and we were breaking up. I'm not sure who it was, but somebody leaked our breakup to the media. A few days after Jingle Ball, Josh asked me to go to lunch at my favorite spot in Laguna Beach, and I agreed. I wanted things to remain amicable. At lunch he was asking random strangers and tourists to take our photo, something out of the ordinary for Josh to do. He begged me to post one of the photos on social media. I knew he only wanted to contradict what the media was saying, to save face.

With Josh gone, I faced a new kind of breakup—the one my daughters would have to experience. I wrestled with how to delicately explain why he would no longer be a part of our lives. I never wanted Kins and Char to experience a loss like

It broke my heart to see the girls have to go through change, but their natural joy and resilience, even as kids, persevered through it all.

this. My intention was for them to have a loving stepfather who would be in their lives forever. But having a completely transparent adult conversation with a four- and two-year-old wasn't all that possible. They were too young to comprehend the complications of our relationship and why it couldn't work. I knew I'd have to explain this to them in a way they could understand.

After I picked the girls up from school, I let them know Josh's dog, Sabel, wasn't feeling very well so Josh had to take her back to Atlanta where the dog's doctor was, so Sabel could see her doctor. This seemed like a reasonable way to explain why Josh would be gone for the time being. Kins was old enough to understand Josh had to leave to take care of his dog. Neither of the girls seemed to be affected by the news. With the holidays coming up I knew there would be lots of distractions, with the arrival of family and Santa Claus. I knew I had some time to ease them into the new normal. It wasn't until after the holidays that the girls started asking questions. I began to let them FaceTime with Josh a few times in the months to follow so he could gradually fade into the background. I felt it was far better than having him suddenly disappear from their lives forever.

Josh's mom called, for what I was hoping would be compassion or motherly advice. Her call was driven by neither of those things. Instead, thirty minutes after Josh and I broke up, his mom wanted to discuss what our official statement to the media would be. She also made a point to mention that while Josh already had a bad reputation with nothing to lose, my reputation was good, and if I dared to say anything bad about him, it could easily be ruined. I couldn't believe what I was hearing. I wondered, *Is she threatening me?* This was the same woman who said she couldn't wait to be a grandmother to my children, the same way Josh said he couldn't wait to be a family man. I felt fooled by them both. Was anything either of them said ever genuine or real? In this case the apple surely didn't fall far from the tree. I hung up on her before I said something I'd later regret and thanked my lucky stars she'd never be my mother-in-law.

I have only had my heart broken one time and that was by Josh. I never wholeheartedly thought that my ex-husband was the love of my life. But with Josh, I really thought, *This is it.* I think Josh also hurt me the most because he promised me all these things, and I believed him. When things he said weren't adding up, I felt betrayed. I think he wants to be perceived as the person he says he is: the God-loving, charitable, sweet-hearted, good ol' boy. I think image is very important to Josh. He said that he didn't want to be on television; he was only there to find love. Meanwhile he's done something like twelve other television shows. He claimed to be a homebody who doesn't like going to bars. But then TMZ posts a video of him drunkenly trying to make out with a girl. I was together with him for six months (seems like six years), let him get close to my children, moved him into my house, made him part of my family—and I never really knew who he was.

I think that's the one relationship that really just changed me as a person for the good and for the bad. I'm much smarter now when it comes to determining someone's character. I have trust issues. It takes a lot for me to believe someone when they say, "Oh, I love kids." A voice goes off in my head that says, *Do you really?* It's easy for someone to say the right things. It goes the other way too. I can sit there on a first date and say I'm a great cook and I only use organic ingredients, when in reality I order Postmates every other day. At first the guy would think *This is great—she is exactly what I'm looking for!* Then later down the road he'd see the real me ordering takeout all the time and think *Wait a second; this isn't what I signed up for.*

It's our duty as decent people to honestly represent ourselves. They say there's a lid to every container, which means there is no need to lie because someone out there is perfectly suited for each of us. Even Josh.

The Rose: Stop Kissing Frogs!

If he doesn't turn into your prince, stop kissing him. Josh's behavior was very frog-like; there were control issues, more than a few untruths told, plus other red flags along the way. (Not to mention Andi Dorfman *wrote a whole book* about his jealous, self-serving ways.) And what did I do? I kept kissing him, hoping he'd turn into a prince!

I knew Josh was kind of controlling when we were filming, but the second we got home from the show he went full throttle. He would give me a hard time when I wanted to talk to my close friends. I would even have to wait for him to go to the gym so I could call my best friend Lauren—or even my mom! He didn't approve of my childhood friends or my neighbors, who used to casually drop by pre-Josh. He pressured me to unfollow certain people on social media (so sorry, Nick Viall), told me what I could and couldn't wear, and even tried to change my flight itinerary behind my back when I was on that girls' trip to Tahoe. When I caught him peeking beneath the bathroom door to make sure I wasn't texting anyone, I finally realized this shouldn't be considered normal relationship behavior. I learned that if it ribbits, hops, and jumps like a frog, it's a freaking frog, and I should stop kissing it—immediately!

The Thorns

- There's a difference between what people say and how they act. On *Bachelor in Paradise*, people can go on and pretend to be whomever they want to portray. Same goes for real life. People can say they want this and that, when truly they don't want a real relationship and they don't believe in marriage. Whether on national TV or a low key first date, you should impress your partner and present the best side of yourself, but you don't want to lie.
- Make sure they know who you are. If a guy I'm with truly thinks I'm up to no good, he doesn't know me. Someone who takes the time to know you will like you for who you are. If you're fun, caring, and loyal, they will appreciate those values.
- Your partner needs to respect *your* needs, even as basic as your sleep. If I could rewind time and pick out one moment I should have ended things with Josh, I would pick the Tree

House incident. He didn't care that I needed sleep; it was all about what he wanted.

- Anger issues: big red flag. If someone flies off the handle from every little thing, it's sure to be a rough road ahead. A great partner is someone who can keep their cool and have a calm, reasonable conversation about anything—especially when they're upset.
- Don't apologize for things that aren't your fault. If you start blaming yourself or making excuses for your partner, you're not in a healthy place.
- Does he regularly get into altercations with other people? No rose. Josh had a hard time being social or even making friends in general. I noticed early on how he often rubbed people the wrong way. Rather than explaining his intentions, Josh would get very defensive and angry, almost always allowing things to escalate into a big confrontation. Because I was on his arm, I would get roped into his problems with other people, and let me tell you, that was no fun.
- Know the difference between something you can work through versus a definite deal breaker. I like to say, "You can work through something, not someone."
- Iffy communication skills and other similar issues can be smoothed out as long as both people are willing to work on it. But you can't change a person or their character.
- If someone lies and doesn't care how you feel from the beginning, they aren't going to wake up one day and care.

Chapter Six

Party of One, Plus Two

*L*OOKING BACK, I REALIZE I've never had an easy, normal relationship. I've always been with guys who haven't trusted me, weren't very nice, and had very little patience. It shouldn't have been a surprise to me when things didn't work out. I started noticing when talking to most of my girlfriends about their previous relationships, they'd usually say, "He was a really good guy, but things just didn't work out for us." I looked back on my serious relationships and could really only say, "He was such an asshole." I'm totally accountable for allowing that to happen. In my next relationship, if he were to become an ex, I wanted to have fond feelings toward him after all was said and done. I kept this in mind as I started to consider dating again.

After I sent Josh packing, it hit me hard that being a mom means you cannot even consider, let alone accept, a hot and cold relationship. Before becoming a mother, it was more of a choice because the only person who would suffer from a separation would be me. But now, a breakup affects my girls, too. There's a big difference between being a single woman and being a single parent. Everyone has their own set of rules, so by no means am I claiming to have the best—or even the right—ones. These are just the rules I've developed for dating as a single mom, and they work for me.

Everyone Has an Opinion

People have left the nastiest comments on my social media. "Trashy," "terrible mom," and "bad influence" are only a few of the insults they've leveled at me. While I might be known to the public for being on a dating show, that part plays no role in my real life. It's not as if I'm parading men through my house. In fact, only two boyfriends besides my ex-husband have ever met my daughters. One I was engaged to and the other I dated for a long time. I waited until we were committed to each other before introducing him to the girls. Nobody knows what happens behind the closed doors of your home, but someone is always going to have an opinion about it. I've learned to tune out the noise and continue doing what I know is best for my family.

Be in Both Places

When I signed on to do *The Bachelor* and *Bachelor in Paradise*, I was aware the producers were going to collect everyone's phones before shooting. Part of my agreement with production was that I'd get to FaceTime with my daughters every single day. If they wouldn't agree to those terms, I simply wouldn't have gone. Opportunities will arise when, as a mom, you wonder if it's okay to sleep away for the night or go on a little trip. Luckily there's this thing called technology that allows us to stay connected at all times, which has really helped me when it comes to allowing myself to be Amanda while still being Mom.

That said, my ex-husband has the girls every other weekend, so I do plan the majority of my events so that I'm away when the girls are with their dad. Additionally, certain life events, such as taking them to their first day of school, making sure the tooth fairy stops by our house when someone loses a tooth, and witnessing a special recital will always take precedence over any opportunity that comes my way.

Timing Is Everything

Finding time to date is especially difficult when yours isn't the only schedule to work around. With kids, you have to factor in school, dance rehearsals, play dates, and birthday parties, in addition to work, grocery shopping, laundry, cleaning, and everything in between. When the girls and I have downtime together, I savor every second! The last thing I'd even consider is choosing a date, whether it's a first or fourteenth, over spending time with Kins and Char. I would never want them to feel my priorities are anywhere but with them. I've gotten pretty good at scheduling dates and trips on weekends when my girls are at their dad's, after they go to bed (with a babysitter there, of course), or while they're at school. Day dates are great: Why not meet for coffee or brunch?

For times when I need a few days away—moms, you know what I'm talking about—I lean on my support system (aka my parents) for help. After I got divorced, at first I never left the girls' sides, thinking I was a better mom for it. But at the same time, I was miserable because I didn't feel like myself. Truth is, we all need a bit of independence from time to time. It's okay, if not essential, to take a work trip or allow yourself a little vacation here and there. For me, time away allows for self-reflection and deep thinking. I come back reenergized and clear-headed, and ultimately a better mom.

No Netflix and Chill

Some moms might be comfortable bringing a guy home after a great date as long as the kids are sleeping, but that has never been okay for me. I've seen enough rom-coms to know how that story ends. The kids could wake up at any time and discover there's a stranger in the house, or worse. I want the girls to know our house belongs to us. Having random guys over while they're asleep would kind of feel disrespectful to them. Our home is their safe space, where they should always feel secure and know what to expect. Besides, it's not the example I want to set for my daughters, and I'd like to be the kind of mom who practices what I preach to them.

Mom.com

When I was online dating, I was always upfront on my profile about being a mom. Granted, anyone could Google me and figure it out, but even if I wasn't in the public eye, I'd be straight up about it. Why hide that you have kids if they're going to find out eventually anyway? Plus, putting it out there weeds out the ones who aren't into kids. Ain't nobody got time for that.

It was clear to me that if someone didn't want this (amazing— haha) package deal, then it wasn't a loss for me.

Quit Playing Games with My Heart—No, Seriously

Since my failed engagement, I have basically zero tolerance for drama or games. I used to excuse wishy-washy behavior and wait it out, thinking the guy would change. Now I don't want to waste time on someone who isn't anything but sure about me or us. The old Amanda who used to sweep red flags under the rug has tossed her broomstick for good. If I see red, they see the door. End of story.

The Good Ones Will Wait

Being on sexually charged dating shows sort of normalized moving fast for me. It was typical and even encouraged to make out with the Bachelor even if you hadn't gone on an official first date. The fantasy suite, a romantic overnight together, is offered up while the Bachelor is still dating multiple women. I used to rush and jump into relationships head first. I take things a lot more slowly now. Since being on these shows, I have concluded that casual dating doesn't equate to sex. As soon as I started making dates wait longer for a first kiss, the ones who weren't right fell by the wayside. I'm currently dating someone who waited ten dates for our first kiss. It felt so right, much more than it has in the past, to wait for that kiss. I believe our ability to see things for what they are gets foggy once physical closeness comes into the picture. Waiting gives you more time to develop an emotional connection, which is far more rare than sexual chemistry. Enjoying someone's company without it being sexual says a lot.

This rule doesn't only apply to single moms, but it's especially important for us because we need to be even choosier when it comes to who comes into our lives. The last thing I want to do is put the girls through another breakup. If a guy is worth a shot, he'll wait for me to decide he's worth kissing—or more.

Hold the Labels

When it comes time for my girls to date (pray for me), I want the girls to not make the same mistakes I did by rushing into relationships. I wouldn't want to normalize always having a new "boyfriend," so therefore 1 made it a rule to not refer to anyone as my boyfriend until they are. If you're excited about a new guy you really like, your kids aren't the ones to glow to; that's what adult friends are for. I think the right time to tell them there's a special person in your life is right around the time you're about to introduce them. That way they are able to process the idea of this new person and adjust.

The Big Decision

I treat introducing a guy to your kids as a big deal because it *is* a very big deal. Once you've introduced a new person to your children, there's no turning back. I felt incredibly irresponsible after allowing Ben (and the cameras) to spend a beach day with my girls. It must have been confusing for their young minds. It was a loud and clear parenting lesson for me. There's no ticking time bomb forcing you to introduce them, so why the hurry? I say take all the time you need or want.

Before introducing my current boyfriend to my girls, I paid close attention to him for four months. How does he treat strangers? Is he patient with people? How does he do in stressful situations? Is he sweet and kind? Can he be fun and silly? Does he like being around children? I discovered the answers to all these questions, and I liked them. He expressed excitement but didn't put an ounce of pressure on me to meet Kins and Char. I knew he was different from the others. Once I felt zero hesitation, I gladly introduced my ladies to my man.

Welcome Party

I always knew the best way for my girls to meet someone new would be outside of the house in a neutral place. I wanted the experience to be just as fun and exciting for them as it would be for us. Places like theme parks, the beach, a painting studio, or the playground make kids feel open and happy. I wouldn't want to take them somewhere like a sit-down dinner or a stranger's house where they might feel uncomfortable or trapped. Hosting the big introduction somewhere light and playful takes the pressure off everyone.

You're the Parent

A big thing for me is making sure my guy knows he's not there to discipline or nanny. I'm not looking for someone else to

The girls' needs come first no matter what.

parent or police my kids. They have two parents who set the rules and order. When it comes to my relationship, I need a partner for me who also loves my children. I knew before I started dating I'd set the expectations and boundaries with my future significant other, letting him know, when it comes to my kids, he's there to love, entertain, play, and support.

It's Okay to Cry

As a mom you always want to be a happy and positive role model around your kids. When you're going through a breakup or a bad day, you don't want them to see you having a weak moment. Looking back, I bottled up way too much around my girls. It's healthy to let your children know when you're feeling sad but also reassure them everything will be okay.

Ex, But Not Really

My ex-husband and I have been through a lot. While it's true we had a rocky past, we've since found a nice place where we can lovingly co-parent. We are in constant communication about the girls, and we frequently have dinner together with them, as a family. Anyone who comes into my life will have to accept that my ex, the father of my daughters, will always be in the picture. I no longer put up with jealousy or animosity when it comes to us communicating or seeing each other for birthday parties or family dinners. It's our special relationship and if someone wants to be cool with me, they'll have to be cool with him, too.

Chapter Seven

Have Kids, Will Travel

$\mathcal{S}$INCE GAINING MY CONFIDENCE BACK as a single woman and mother, I've felt inspired and motivated to explore the world well beyond my comfort zone. It started with *The Bachelor* and really took off from there. Once I had a taste of the travel bug, I was off and running. Sometimes I travel alone, but often I travel with Kinsley and Charlie. I understand this chapter isn't for everyone, so if you don't have kids and feel this doesn't apply to you, it won't hurt my feelings if you skip ahead. For the rest of you still here, I wanted to share some of what I've learned over the years about traveling with little ones.

When she was a baby, Kinsley had been on a couple of flights to St. Louis to visit my parents, so by the time Charlie came around, Kins was a somewhat seasoned flyer. When Charlie turned two, I decided to roll the dice and take them both to Missouri. This wasn't my first rodeo, so I made sure to pack a carry-on full of goodies to entertain both of the kids.

Coloring books, reading books, dolls, snacks, iPads . . . you name it, we had it. The afternoon flight there went shockingly well. I was super proud and happy with how smoothly things went. I spoke too soon.

The flight home was a completely different story. After a few days of traveling, sleeping in a hotel, and dealing with a slight time change, Charlie was exhausted. As soon as we boarded our flight back home, she fell asleep, and she stayed asleep a majority of the flight. And then she woke up. The last hour or so of the flight might as well have lasted five hours. Char was so restless and cranky. I was just desperately trying to get her to sit down and watch a movie, but she was *not* having it. After spilling an entire bag of Goldfish crackers on the floor of the plane and karate kicking the seat in front of her (sorry, guy in front of us), I knew this was going to be the longest hour of our lives. My anxiety was kicking in big time. I was so stressed. We were those people—the people everyone on the plane hates.

Finally, in a moment of desperation, I let her walk around the aisle of the plane. This seemed to be the only thing keeping her from screaming, spilling, or kicking the poor guy in front of us. From the corner of my eye, I noticed the lady in the row behind us watching Char and giving her a kind of mean smirk. After a few minutes of trotting up and down the aisle, Charlie started whining for her doll. The smirking lady behind us removed her headphones, looked little Charlie in the eye, and said to her, "I think it's time for you to take a nap."

Now, I know most of you have never seen this side of me and, given my typically sunny disposition, most probably don't even know it exists. But in this moment, my inner mama bear came out. All my stress, tension, and anxiety let loose on this lady on an airplane. I don't remember much of what I said because I was so flustered, but I do remember telling her, "If you have a problem with how my daughter is behaving, you can say something to me. She is two years old. Don't talk to my daughter. Don't even look at my daughter." I remember I was shaking the rest of the plane ride home, feeling so upset over the way this lady had spoken to Charlie.

Look, I get it. When you're on the other side of this equation, kids can be less than ideal to have on your flight. They cry, they scream, they kick your seat. To be honest, I am often less than enthused to be sitting next to or behind a toddler on a trip when I'm not with my own. But I can assure you their parents hate it even more than you! When your child starts misbehaving on a plane, it's the most stressful thing in the world. It's so embarrassing, and on top of that, you feel so helpless. You know everyone is wishing you'd take a dive out of the emergency exit. So, if you're a non-parent reading this (if you're still here), take it easy on the parents and don't roll your eyes or make them feel worse about a bad situation. And most definitely don't be rude to their children!

Since this flight from hell, Charlie and Kinsley have been on many flights, and I'm ecstatic to say it has gotten way better. I've definitely learned a lot about how to make traveling with kids much easier. I'm not going to lie, it is never totally easy—but *easier*.

First and foremost, nonstop flights are 100 percent necessary! If nonstop isn't an option, try to go for the least amount of stops possible. Especially if you want them to sleep.

If you're going somewhere that's a three-hour flight or less, I recommend flying in the early afternoon. That way you're not waking your kids up early to head to the airport, so they'll be well rested and less cranky.

For flights over four hours, we love a red-eye! I know traveling way past bedtime (all our bedtimes) seems a little scary to think about, but it works out. I'll talk to my kids beforehand to get them excited about wherever we are going. When we get on the plane, they know that it's time to sleep because, as soon as they wake up, we'll be at this exciting place! Obviously, if you're traveling somewhere far enough for an overnight flight, there's going to be a time difference, and when you land it's already morning. I plan ahead for an early check-in and go straight to the hotel room, where the kids can take a nap for two hours or so. This way we are all rested and still have most of the day ahead of us. I try to never plan activities the day we arrive or even the day after. I like to make those the relaxing days to settle in, let the kids rest when they need to, and get them adjusted to the time change.

Entertaining kids on long flights can be tricky. They get bored so easily, so having a variety of options is key. If your plane has in-seat television screens, they can rent a movie, which, depending on their age, will help pass some of the time.

I always download a ton of games onto their iPads and make sure they're fully charged. Remember that sometimes there is no WiFi in flight (I learned this the hard way on our trip to Turks and Caicos recently) so make sure everything is accessible offline. Other must-haves are coloring books, crayons, and lots of snacks but not too many drinks, so you're not getting up to use the restroom every thirty minutes.

I've heard so many people recommend giving kids cough medicine before a trip to knock 'em out. I'd never done it because it didn't feel right, but, just in case of desperation, I did buy some as a backup for a long trip we took a few months ago. I saw another parent giving his daughter some cough medicine right before we were about to board and thought, *This should be interesting*. His daughter cried and threw tantrums the *entire* flight as mine colored peacefully in their seats (thank goodness). It made me so glad I didn't go against my instincts to try this method. I strongly encourage parents not to go this route. Being extremely exhausted + overstimulated = a bad combination.

Finding the right hotel is another thing to consider when you travel with kids. You definitely want to make sure everything is kid friendly. Staying at a hotel or resort that's not entirely kid friendly can cause a parent a lot of stress. If you're on vacation, you want to be able to enjoy yourself and not be worried about your children misbehaving at a five-star restaurant. At the same time, you don't want to be having all your dinners at a place like Chuck E. Cheese every night. A kid-friendly hotel will have an option that is perfectly in between. Rather than people growling at you as they try to enjoy a romantic anniversary dinner, you'll be surrounded by other parents who give you the "much respect" nod when your kid eats spaghetti sans hands on the floor because she decided to be a puppy that night.

On that note, before booking a reservation at a hotel I always check the menus at the restaurants and room service to make sure there are options my picky kids will eat but also dishes that I can enjoy, too.

One tip for parents with babies and small children: Most travel destinations have companies that rent out gear such as car seats, strollers, cribs, swings, activity gyms, bouncy seats, humidifiers, and even things like beach umbrellas and toys. Why go through the drama of lugging that stuff across the country when you can have it delivered right to you upon arrival? Total life saver!

Try to look for a hotel with a kids' club or program. A kids' club is a designated area where you can drop your kids off for a few hours while you have dinner or go swimming on your own. They usually have great activities or programs for children to enjoy, so the kids are happy to be there. Even if you're not planning to use it, it's nice to have the option just in case you get overwhelmed and need some time to yourself. These clubs are usually a highlight of the trip for the kids.

Kid-friendly options aside, I also like to see what kinds of activities and amenities the hotel has for adults only. Some parents feel guilty thinking about this aspect on a family trip, but I feel it is very important that you all get to enjoy your vacation. That's when the kids' club comes into play. Get a massage, enjoy a grown-up meal, or even take a nap!

I always appreciate a designated kid pool or a park where they can play while I get a chance to lay back and relax, while keeping an eye on them, of course. If you decide to stay somewhere that has activities for kids that require you to be hands-on the whole time, you might feel like it's less of a vacation for you because you're constantly running around with your children. Because let's be real, a vacation with kids should just be called a trip.

On our last trip to Hawaii, we stayed somewhere with a modest park and a kids' pool. They had some low-key activities for kids (lei making, beach treasure hunts, etc.), but it was mainly a relaxing resort for adults. I bought us all day passes to another hotel meant more for families that featured a massive water park. We all had so much fun, but I couldn't help but think I would have been exhausted if we had stayed there and the kids wanted to do that every day of our vacation. Of course, you want your kids to have the best time ever. But you're on vacation too, and there's nothing worse than leaving a trip even more tired and stressed than you were before you got there. You shouldn't need a vacation after your vacation. It's all about balance.

Speaking of our trip to Hawaii, that's hands down our favorite place to travel! We really love anywhere tropical, though: the Bahamas, Turks and Caicos, you name it. It's so relaxing, and the kids can be free and run around. Taking

Traveling with two toddlers can be a nightmare, but
it's moments like these that are irreplaceable.

them somewhere that has more of a city vibe seems a little
more restricted when it comes to kids. I like to go somewhere
that doesn't require a lot of driving, where the kids can feel
free to run and play. Our first trip to Maui was our favorite, and
we didn't even do much in terms of parks or kiddie pools. We
found turtles down at the beach, swam at the pool every day,
and ate snow cone after snow cone. Sometimes it's not necessary to go crazy jam-packing activities into every day. As it
usually is, less is often more.

One question I get asked a lot is how I manage to take so many photos of my kids on vacation. I make taking photos of us a priority to look back on now but also so the kids can look back on them when they're older. I usually travel with someone else, like my mom or my sister. Usually they'll help out when it comes to taking photos of me with the girls, especially the candid ones, which are always my personal favorite. But more times than you'd think, I use a self-timer! You don't need

It's amazing to be able to look back at these photos, and I can't wait for the day I can share stories with Kins and Char.

a photographer following you around on vacation to get great photos. A good old self-timer and a folio case are seriously a game changer. There's an easy-to-use self-timer app on the iPhone. I'll find and use anything to prop my phone up against to capture a shot. A table, car, or tree . . . you name it! Sometimes it takes a few trials and errors, but once you get the hang of it, it's easy.

Now, getting your kids to smile and pose for you is the hard part. That's why candid photos have become my favorite. I never want to force my kids to take photos when they don't want to (Charlie hates taking photos). Sometimes it helps to bribe them with a little candy or ice cream or some kind of treat. Come on, we all do it! Kinsley is at the age now of liking to take photos because she knows how much she loves looking back at them later. It's so sweet and melts my heart. I hope Charlie gets there soon!

I don't think anyone can ever master being on the move with little ones. There will be times when your kids cry on the plane no matter what you offer them. They're likely to kick the seat in front of them or refuse to sleep. There are going to be nights when you have to cancel dinner reservations because it's just impossible to pull everything and everyone together. And that's okay. All of it. I've learned it's best to try to embrace the chaos. Sometimes those moments somehow make for the best memories!

Chapter Eight

Paradise, Interrupted

*A*FTER CALLING OFF MY ENGAGEMENT to Josh, I took a year-long break from dating. Truthfully, for five months after the breakup, we would fly out to see each other, secretly trying to work things out. Even though he was controlling and difficult, I felt pressured to try to make things work with him because he did get so close to my daughters. The guilt was almost as severe as splitting the kids up from their real dad. Ultimately, it just couldn't work. Josh just wasn't the guy I hoped he could be.

That breakup hit me the hardest because I truly thought I found my person, and I had put it out there in front of what felt like the whole world. I cringe when I think about the family photo session Josh and I did with my girls. It's embarrassing to look back at the degree to which I fought for things to work out.

After things ended with Josh, my mind was focused solely on my girls. Second to them, I was doing some serious soul searching. I took a good look within myself to recognize where I'd gone wrong in my choices and how I could do better in the future. I spent a lot of time taking walks by myself, listening to my inner voice.

About a year later, when the opportunity to return to season four of *Bachelor in Paradise* came up, I was skeptical. The last time I was on the show I got myself into a very unhealthy relationship. I felt as though I'd wasted my chance on *Paradise* because I didn't pay attention to red flags or listen to the warnings. It was as if everyone was screaming, "The inside of that house is on fire!" but I stupidly ran right through the front door. Plus, I can tell you that public breakups are a thousand times worse than private ones.

A quiet voice inside me said, *Hey, this almost worked last time. Why not try it again?* Just because I blew my last opportunity didn't guarantee I'd do it again. I felt like this was a second chance to go and make better decisions. I knew I wasn't going to get engaged again. If there was someone there for me at *Paradise*, I wanted to take it a lot more slowly. This time I'd date on my real-life timeline as opposed to the show's timeline. One caveat for me was whether or not Josh would also be participating on the show. If he was going to be on *Paradise*, I definitely was not. With a firm promise from production that Josh would not be on season four and a small glimmer of hope that I might meet someone amazing, I decided to go for it.

The first time I was on *Paradise*, I was the very first person to arrive on day one. It was a nice advantage being able to meet everyone as they arrived. This time I was the last person to get there. All participants are kept in the dark as far as who all is coming to *Paradise*. That's part of the fun! As I made my way down the stairs, the first person I saw was Corinne. We had met the year before at a concert in L.A. and had a good time together. It was a relief to see someone I sort of knew. Corinne, in a pretty pink dress, was soaked head to toe from jumping in the pool fully clothed. Typically, we girls try to look our best on the first day, so it took me aback that Corinne would be so casual and carefree, without makeup, perfect hair, or even dry clothes. When Corinne saw me, she called out my name and started running toward the stairs. She almost fell down, which made me realize right away just how wasted she was. But she wasn't the only one. The rest of the cast was also already very drunk. Still, Corinne was the drunkest of the bunch. If you look at the cast photo taken that day, you'll notice I'm pretty much holding her upright.

While most of us were still getting to know one another, Corinne and DeMario were all over each other. From my perspective it was definitely mutual and in good fun. I saw Corinne and DeMario make their way to the pool as the rest of us hung out on the beach. I was bummed there weren't any of the girls from my last season. I didn't know anybody there, girls or guys. I tried to keep an upbeat demeanor, but truthfully, I felt a little lost. I noticed Corinne and DeMario move from the pool to the hot tub but didn't think much of it. Nobody was paying close attention to them. We were all too busy checking each other out to pay them any mind.

Since Corinne was the only girl I kind of knew, we ended up spending the most time together. Over the next couple of days of filming, she kept getting pulled aside by producers, but I didn't know why. I thought maybe she was being a diva asking for special treatment or voicing her concern about how she'd be portrayed. The truth was, Corinne had a serious boyfriend when she came on the show. She and her boyfriend had an understanding that she wasn't there to hook up with anyone but rather promote herself and her brand. From the start she was upfront with the producers, telling them she had no intentions of hooking up with any of the guys. But then on the first day she had sex with DeMario in the pool. I think Corinne's biggest concern was if and how her boyfriend was going to find out what happened between her and DeMario. That was my guess at the time as to why she kept talking to producers on the side. None of us had any idea what that tryst would turn into.

The night that production shut down started out like any other. We had a cast cocktail hour before separating the guys from the girls, as they always do. I was nervous at not having connected with any of the guys. I didn't know what would happen at that rose ceremony. I wasn't attracted to anyone there. I wasn't even sure if I wanted to stay, but then again that's the thing about *Paradise*. You never know who might show up the next day.

Chris Harrison, our host, called everybody in for a chat when suddenly and simultaneously the camera crew put their cameras down. Chris said to us, "This is not fake. The cameras are off." We were all very confused, feeling left in the dark as to why production stopped. We had no idea why what happened between DeMario and Corinne should cause cameras to stop rolling. The general consensus with the cast was that Corinne got too drunk and did something with DeMario that she regretted. Maybe she blamed production for not stopping them, knowing how drunk she was? We'd later find out it was a producer who caused filming to stop because the producer felt uncomfortable about what had transpired. The producer was concerned Corinne was too drunk to give consent. I felt at the time that the whole thing was being blown way out of proportion. Yes, Corinne was drunk, but she was not passed out or close to it. She was very much present, from what I could tell. At the end of the day, we are all adults who make our own decisions, good or bad.

The next three days were like being on a real vacation. We got to relax, get a tan, and swim while we awaited the fate of the show. As nice as it was to be relaxing, I still felt haunted by everything that happened there the year before. I didn't think going back to *Paradise* would be difficult for me, but once I arrived the memories came rushing back. Every room, every inch of that resort, was attached to a memory with Josh. It was especially hard spending time on the beach where we got engaged. It was all still very fresh in my mind. I sometimes sneaked off camera to cry. But still, I was motivated to create new memories on *Paradise*. I wasn't sure if we were cancelled, postponed, or what.

The producers pulled me aside and told me that since I have kids I could leave if I wanted to. They made it pretty clear they weren't sure what would happen with the show either. I definitely didn't want to spend another day away from my girls if I didn't have to, so I decided to leave. I told the producers to call me if they picked back up and I'd make the two-hour flight back. Corinne and I were the first to leave. We flew home together. She was also very confused about what was going on and why it was happening. To this day I still don't think anyone really knows what happened. Corinne's boyfriend picked her up from the airport, which made me believe he didn't know anything about what just happened. He soon would. Everyone would. None of us had any idea just how big the media would blow this up. We knew it was a big deal behind the scenes because production never suspends filming for anything. But we never would have thought it would be the top story on every media outlet. When the news broke, it seemed every outlet had a different story, one more scandalous than the next. I thought for sure the show was done and never coming back.

I don't know who started the rumor that DeMario was at fault for what happened between him and Corinne in the pool. Seeing the media portray him as a possible rapist was disgusting and hard to take. Nobody from the cast felt DeMario did anything wrong. Some of us suspected Corinne of spreading these damaging rumors about DeMario because she didn't want her boyfriend to find out she'd willingly had sex with someone else. But I no longer believe this to be true. I think it was fabricated by the rumor mill to make a bigger story out of it. I was glad when the public retracted its claws from DeMario after realizing it was a consensual encounter. The assumption it wasn't definitely wasn't fair or true.

I was shocked when production called less than a few weeks later to say we'd be returning to film the rest of season four of *Paradise*. They didn't have us reshoot anything. Instead, they addressed the scandal on the air and had us pick up right where we left off. While we were on a break, a lot of people kept in touch and developed relationships off camera. These relationships led to a few hookups and some unexpected drama upon return.

As viewers saw, Lacey was absolutely obsessed with Daniel. They met once and apparently FaceTimed occasionally before the show resumed, and that was enough for Lacey to know Daniel was the one for her. She mentioned that *Bachelor in Paradise* was their chance to be together. I heard from another participant she had an engagement ring picked out before she even went on the show. Suffice it to say, Lacey came off more than just a little nutty. She went in way too hard. If you go into *Paradise* desperate to get engaged, that's exactly how you're going to come off. And the same goes for real life. People can sense desperation. It isn't cute on anyone. The best attitude to have in any situation is if you meet someone, that would be cool. If not, you'll be a-okay.

The same kind of thing happened with Jasmine, who—let's just say it—went crazy on *Paradise*. Jasmine became super aggressive toward Matt after going on just one date. Immediately she was all in at 100 percent. It's easy to get ahead of yourself on *Paradise* because you go on this show with the expectation of falling in love. Everything happens really fast. People really do get engaged after three weeks on the show or at least leave the show in serious relationships. Look at Raven and Adam, for example. It worked for them! And they're so happy. Adam is one of the rare gems on the show. And Raven is one of the greatest girls I know. They both got really lucky to have found each other on the show.

The second you go on a good date, you're like, *Oh my gosh, it's happening! I'm going to have what Raven and Adam have!* It's hard not to let that excitement turn into possessiveness. I've wondered if Matt would have been more interested in Jasmine if she had played it cool. I completely sympathized with her disappointment. When it doesn't work out the way you hoped, you're crushed, because you only get a few chances on *Paradise*. But in the real world, of course, it doesn't work like that. We have an unlimited amount of times to get it right. Nobody is trying to squeeze your love life into a short season.

Nobody crushed harder than Dean on that season. Crushed Kristina's heart, that is. To be honest, I really like Dean, and I felt badly for him. He was portrayed as a player or a jerk on the show when that isn't who he is at all. He was fresh off the emotional rollercoaster of filming Rachel's season of *The Bachelorette*, where he'd made it pretty far. He walked right into shooting *Paradise* where basically every girl was interested in him. Dean is a cute guy, but I don't think he was used to getting the level of attention he was receiving from all these sexy, hot, older women who wanted him bad. I think he tried to handle the situation with Kristina and D-Lo as best as he

could, but at the end of the day he was young and temptation like that is hard for anyone to handle. He didn't handle
it well. In fact, I think he handled it pretty poorly, but again,
I think that was due to his young age and lack of experience,
not to him being a bad guy. He is a nice guy with a good heart.
Unlike a lot of the guys who go on the show for attention,
not caring about hurting anyone's feelings, I believe Dean was
there for the right reasons.

Robby and I did not hit it off right away. When we first
met, I thought he was the biggest douchebag ever. Then he
reached out to me over the break, and we started talking here
and there. I decided maybe he wasn't all that bad. When we
returned to *Paradise*, I saw him as a cool guy friend, someone
I could hang out with. As time passed, I grew lonely for com-
panionship while we were filming because I didn't have any of
my girlfriends there. That's how I saw Robby, as my only friend
in *Paradise*. I wasn't blind to the fact Robby was trying to make
something happen between the two of us. If you watch the
episodes, you'll see he tried to kiss me twenty or so times, and
every time I denied him.

Eventually, the producers began encouraging me to move
forward with Robby. I wasn't there for a free vacation, after
all. Viewers tune in to witness romantic connections, not to
watch me get a tan. I caved and the kissing began. One thing
led to another and I started to let Robby out of the friend zone.
Although we were what I'd call casually dating, I never fully
believed there would be a future between us. The things I ask
for in a relationship, such as commitment and loyalty, would

never come from Robby. Whereas Josh would pretend he was someone different than who he was, Robby was very straight-forward about his intentions. Robby was honest in telling me he loved partying and he'd never give it up for anyone. He also admitted he'd always want attention from other girls. I'd been down this road before and didn't like where it took me. For those reasons, I broke up with him on the show before things got serious.

When you leave a show like *Paradise*, you remain close with the people you experienced it with because only they understand what you went through. Robby and I reconnected when we got home. Although we did hang out for a while, I never introduced him to my kids. He was pushing for us to be something more, but I never trusted him enough to let that happen. To me, we were just having fun and enjoying each other's company.

Six weeks post-*Paradise*, when it came time to film the reunion show, Robby wanted to announce us as a couple, which took me aback because we really weren't a couple. At that point, I hadn't even seen him in weeks. When a fan direct messaged me a photo of Robby kissing another girl at a con-cert, I was further convinced he wasn't truly interested in any type of relationship or commitment. The night before the show, Robby called my hotel to discuss what we were going to say about our relationship status. I was very honest and clear with him when I explained we had barely talked in weeks, that I knew he was out in clubs kissing other girls, and I wasn't interested in fabricating a relationship. He asked if we could say that we are still hanging out and seeing where it goes. I said absolutely not. I felt his motivation was to look good and get more airtime. It made me laugh to think of the desperate measures to which some people will go to gain more Instagram followers. But I guess that's expected for a "social media expert." That's when I decided, once and for all, to put Robby back in the friend zone where he belonged.

The Rose: Taking a Chance

Do I regret going back to *Paradise* for a second run? Truthfully . . . kind of. I didn't end up meeting anyone special, and I didn't get the same bonding time with my close girlfriends as I did the time before. But I also know that had I not gone, I would have wondered "what if." I'm also glad I allowed myself the chance to create new memories to replace the ones that made me sad. Now when I think of *Paradise* I'm not flooded with memories of Josh. I'm reminded of a bunch of fun times I spent on a beautiful beach making new friends. At the end of the day, I still believe we should always come from a place of yes. Taking chances may or may not go the way we hope, but the chances are always greater when you go for it.

The Thorns

- Don't judge a situation until you get the whole picture. Most of us were guilty of speculating who said and did what with the Corinne and DeMario situation. Had we

129

only waited a few weeks we would have known it wasn't anywhere near what the rumors suggested.

- Let it go for good. Next time I break up with someone because they're not right for me, I'm committing to that choice. Going back and forth with an ex, trying to force something that's not there, is a painful waste of everyone's time.

- Don't be desperate. If you're just dying for a boyfriend, definitely keep that between you and your friends. Nobody wants to be with someone who'd probably settle for anybody else.

- Play it cool. Hitting fast forward after one or two good dates is more likely to send someone running in whatever direction you're not in.

- If you know someone's not for you, don't keep him around purely for entertainment. I let things go way too far with Robby simply because there was no one else to hang out with. This mistake got me caught up in a weird web I wish I hadn't messed with in the first place.

Chapter Nine

Before You Vaycay

*W*HILE MY LOVE LIFE wasn't exactly on point following my second trip to *Paradise*, my vacation style sure was. Since this wasn't my first go, I knew what to expect, what to pack, and how to prepare for my return. It still took a lot of planning and work, but by the second time around, I was a little bit more relaxed and less anxious about the dating aspect of *Paradise*. To be honest, I went into it thinking that if I didn't end up liking someone, at least I could throw on my best bikini and lay out on the beach. Am I right?

Obviously, there are many reasons why going on vacation is so, so beneficial and necessary. Sometimes, you just need to disconnect from work life or your regular routine to recharge and re-inspire yourself. Being able to explore the world through the type of exotic foods you taste, the eclectic people you meet, the interesting places you see, and, of course, the things you get to wear are what make a vacation experience whole. Changing up my typical at-home style and picking out the perfect evening dress for a warm tropical night out or the perfect fluffy coat for a cold winter's night in New York is honestly one of my favorite things about traveling. Living in Orange County I rarely get to bundle up, so I look forward to trips where I get to style myself for someone else's lifestyle. It's fun!

I'm not sure what the norm is when it comes to packing, but I am one to plan my outfits down to every detail. Depending on luggage space, I'll sometimes pack about a dozen extra pieces "just in case." If you read my packing tips in Chapter Three, you'll know that wasn't so much of a luxury on *The Bachelor*, and typically isn't always the way I pack, but I think I have some sort of weird FOMO or something when it comes to vacation style. I want to get every brightly colored, floral printed item in there! Even though my trips are sometimes really short, I do try to fit in the occasional outfit changes from time to time.

Since we're coming fresh from my experience on *Bachelor in Paradise* in my last chapter, I thought it would be a great way to transition into my must-haves for warm-weather destinations.

MUST HAVE: Matching Sets

You'll notice in *Bachelor in Paradise* season four that I wore multiple matching sets, which was one of my best style decisions because it made coordinating outfits so easy! Plus, most matching sets are usually cute tops with flowy bottoms. It gets extremely humid in *Paradise*, so wearing tight clothing actually does nobody any service. Definitely check the humidity levels before your travel plans because that can have a huge effect on what not to wear. Going for anything too binding in a non-breathable fabric ends up being uncomfortably hot and suffocating. When I'm on vacation now, I always make sure that the matching sets I have are made with cool, light, and airy materials. Breathable fabric just feels so much nicer at night when you're cruising around the city—whether that's walking around downtown or just hanging out at the beach.

I also ended up sometimes ditching the top and sporting the bottoms with a cute bikini top or using a one-piece bathing suit as a body suit. Even with a single matching set, I was able to play mix-and-match with all the pieces, allowing one outfit to work as two or three. Best investment when it comes to tropical weather!

MUST HAVE: Day-to-Night Romper

Exploring the nightlife in a completely new city can be so magical. That excitement of finding out what the city has to offer in terms of live music or even having a date night in a small, local corner restaurant can feel adventurous, romantic, and intimate.

I packed several mini dresses for both seasons of *Bachelor in Paradise*, but I came to the conclusion that rompers (especially for the unexpected windy nights) are always the best bet. On the show I had about a minute's notice for one-on-one dates, so last minute that I barely had any time to get ready. Sometimes you'll notice the girls just go in whatever it is they're wearing. The same could happen on any vacation:

Dresses are my favorite because they make you look
put together and are the easiest thing to pack.

The day gets away from you and suddenly you're en route
to a night out. Rompers are the perfect way to appear glam
and dressed up but be extremely comfortable. To elevate the
ensemble from casual to nice, you could swap out flip-flops for

fancier flats or heels and upgrade with a few pieces of jewelry. So easy and fast!

MUST HAVE: Bold Statement Earrings

If you look back on the episodes of *Bachelor in Paradise*, you can see that most of the clothes I wear are neutral colors. I may love the color pink and can be really girly, but when I have the chance to pick between black and any other color, I usually go with black. Call me crazy, but when I went to *Paradise*, I invested in six of the same style earrings from Shashi, all in exuberant and lively colors. I picked out colors I would never wear when it came to my usual everyday clothes, such as yellow, orange, lavender, and luscious emerald green. These bold colors are much more vacation-Amanda than they are the at-home me. Plus, it's a lot easier to pack ten pairs of colorful earrings with a few solid tops than equal amounts of colorful shirts. Nobody would even notice you wore the same shirt twice because they're bedazzled by your bling.

While I'm sometimes not as daring when it comes to my clothes, I'm never afraid to be a little more outgoing when it comes to my earrings. Pair them with a high pony and you've got yourself an effortless look for any occasion.

MUST HAVE: Block-Heeled Sandals

Shoes are the trickiest thing for me when on vacation. First off, my feet (and my fingers) swell when traveling, so sandals with a lot of straps are not always the cutest at the end of the night when my feet look like tiger toes. At home, I'm either a heels or sneakers kind of girl—there's no in between. That said, vacation-Amanda had to learn to adjust due to climate and environment. Heels aren't the smartest choice on holiday. You never know if you'll be cruising on cobblestone or uneven outdoor flooring, not to mention the possibility of sand. My solution? A pair of simple block heels. Thicker, wider heels are easier to walk in, especially in Mexico. I prefer a pair with just a little height (two to three inches), so I know I won't fall flat on my face. I always feel that super high heels on vacation look a bit ridiculous anyway. It's vacation! Leave the stilettos at home.

MUST HAVE: Wide-Brimmed Hat

While, first and foremost, a large hat is a must-have for blocking your face from the sun, which otherwise can cause sunspots and wrinkles (more on this in a bit!), a shady hat can also conceal all the frizziness and flyaway hairs caused by humidity. Talk about an easy fix! This glam accessory is always on trend, and it makes every poolside look a little more elevated. Basically, a wide-brimmed hat is your best friend on every sunny vacation.

MUST HAVE: A Cute Kimono

You can always spot me in a kimono of some sort when I'm on vacation. Even in *Paradise*, for beach cover I wore a long white

Hats are sometimes tricky to pack, but having it protect your skin is
a bonus. I always try to pack at least one that goes with everything.

kimono about which many viewers inquired. I love kimonos
because they work well with a simple outfit like shorts and a
bodysuit but also work as coverups for all styles of swimsuits.

They're easy to pack and look great on all body types. The overall look of a kimono is pretty elegant and chic but also very boho-babe. I'm a fan!

MUST HAVE: Your Beauty Routine on Lock

When it comes to beauty, I like to keep things super minimalistic and casual when I'm at the beach or poolside. There's really no point in fussing over wardrobe or wearing too much makeup because I want most of my time spent in the water as opposed to in front of the mirror. At the same time, I do want to look and feel my best. Luckily, there's a little prep work that can be done before you leave for vacation that does almost all the work for you.

I'm not shy about admitting I have (and love) eyelash extensions. I am also a huge fan of hair extensions. Yes, there is quite a bit of upkeep for both, but the tradeoff is I have less upkeep on a day-to-day basis. Because I'm a mom of two little ones, the time saved by having extensions is priceless. To not have to spend the extra time curling and applying mascara because of my eyelash extensions is good enough reason to keep getting them done. I actually feel like I hardly need makeup at all because they make me feel made up enough. I've had eyelash extensions for years. They haven't damaged my actual lashes because I take care of them by using a nurturing eyelash serum (neuLASH and neuBROW are my go-tos for brows and lashes). It's important to make sure your natural lashes stay strong and healthy to hold onto the extensions. I also regularly take hair vitamins, which are keeping my natural hair shiny and strong enough to hold my wefts.

With all of that being said, when I'm on vacation, it doesn't take me long to get ready because I keep the beauty products to a minimum. I already have my lashes done and my hair looks good, so, oftentimes, I just slather on a tinted moisturizer with SPF, maybe sweep on some neutral-colored eyeshadow, and ditch the eyeliner and mascara. After popping on a tinted lip balm and a smidge of powder, I'm all ready to go with essentially a no-makeup makeup look.

If you're totally anti-eyelash extensions (I have some girl-friends who can't stand them, so I get that they're not for everyone), then I completely recommend a lash lift. If I wasn't wearing eyelash extensions, this would be my second choice. A lift is a two-hour chemical process similar to a perm, that naturally lifts up your lashes and keeps them beautifully curled for six to eight weeks. Most places will even tint them as part of the deal. So essentially you leave looking like you have a coat of mascara on for a few months. Weekly or monthly eye-lash extensions or enhancements can be somewhat costly, but if you're going on a special trip or if it's a special occasion, then this is something I would definitely splurge on!

Wearing less makeup was a milestone for me since I strug-gled with acne when I was younger. It still hasn't completely gone away, but learning about different skincare techniques from my esthetician, Amber, from Facial Lounge in Corona

Del Mar, really changed the way I took care of my skin. I also cut out most dairy and all gluten, which has improved my breakouts tremendously. Just because I'm on vacation doesn't mean my skin is, too. I don't skimp on the skincare products I bring on a trip. With me, I always have:

- Dr. Dennis Gross Peel Pads
- Facial Lounge lathering face wash
- tons and tons of moisturizing sheet masks
- toner (Korean brands generally have the best)
- a thick night cream
- eye cream
- SPF in all my makeup or SPF in my moisturizer if I'm not wearing any makeup
- makeup wipes to get all the dirt and grime from being outdoors all day off my face
- a rosewater mister to hydrate my face from the sun and warmer weather

I also never, ever fall asleep with makeup on, no matter how tired I am or how many drinks I have had; my makeup is always coming off one way or another. It may seem a little high maintenance to bring all those products on vacation with you, but sometimes we forget that our skin goes through so much shock or change when we go from one climate to another. Even the type of water coming from the shower can make a difference. Your skin can definitely feel the weight of the atmosphere, so it's always better to go the extra mile even when on vacation.

Speaking of going the extra mile, I always make sure to get a little spray tan before heading out on vacation to make sure that I'm evenly tan all over before living in a bikini. If I don't have time to get a spray tan, I'll generally go for an at-home tanning lotion like Jergens, Sally Hansen, or St. Tropez.

Also, because by now we've become close friends, I'll get really personal with you: I never shave my bikini area, ever. Instead I always, always go for sugaring over shaving or even waxing. Sugaring is just a gentler, more sanitary, warm, sticky sugar-based substance that pulls and removes your hair. It never burns (like hot wax does) and is a more natural way of removing bikini hair. It's not exactly pain-free, but it's worth the reward. I find what makes sugaring extra worth it is that I don't get razor burns or bumps, and it lasts about four to six weeks. Plus, as a bonus, the more you sugar, the thinner your hair gets over time, too!

Here's my personal pre-vacation checklist for you to consider before your next tropical trip:

- ☐ Eyelash extensions, or a touch-up, or a keratin lash lift, so that you start the vacation fresh with a full set. With lash lifts, give yourself at least twenty-four hours before the trip because you can't get them wet right after the process.
- ☐ Tightening up your hair extensions with your stylist so that they're nice and secure when you're out of town.

- ☐ Spray tan or a self-tanner at home. Get this a few days prior to your actual trip to make sure that it's exactly the shade you want.
- ☐ Sugaring or waxing, depending on what you prefer, but I prefer sugaring. If you absolutely cannot do either, then don't forget to stock up on shaving cream.
- ☐ Gel manicure and pedicure, especially for when you're walking on the beach and wearing open-toed sandals all the time.
- ☐ Get a facial at least one week before your trip. Sometimes, your skin takes at least a week to heal from extractions or from microdermabrasion. A week will also give your skin some time to rest and rejuvenate before being exposed to sunlight.
- ☐ Detox your bod and keep it healthy. Before I became committed to a gluten- and dairy-free lifestyle, I would only do it in preparation for a trip. I really noticed the difference in my skin and body tone. I also put alcohol on the back burner before a trip to avoid the sugar. With the one-two-three punch of taking out gluten, dairy, and sugar, I always feel and look my absolute best. But once I am at my destination and in vacation mode, I allow myself to indulge. What's a vaycay sans margaritas and mojitos anyway?

Chapter Ten

Date Expectations

*T*HE BACHELOR WOULD BE LACKLUSTER without its grandiose dates. Coming on the show, you can expect that your dates will include helicopters, deserted beaches, Jacuzzis covered in rose petals, and other luxurious surprises beyond your wildest dreams. Upon my return to reality, I was reminded that not every date culminates in a private concert with your favorite band. These over-the-top experiences heighten your emotions overall, making you believe this is indeed the best date of your life. I don't only credit the extravagant dates with resulting in extreme feelings. I also attribute falling so quickly to the fact that contestants are separated from their families, friends, television, phones, bills, and so on. Our only focus is our relationships. Nothing else exists at the time. We are all on our best behavior and basically on an all-expenses-paid vacation.

When Josh and I came home from *Paradise*, everything changed. For one, my daughters are my number one priority, so Josh took an instant, nonnegotiable back seat. My ex-husband Nick is also a huge part of my life because we co-parent and make a conscious effort to keep a positive relationship for our girls' sake. Life became a whole lot less about chilling out all day, cuddling by the beach, and going on luxurious dates. Things got real—fast. Real-life dates aren't orchestrated by a production team, and, therefore, you're not going to be swept off your feet every time. I believe the monumental gestures can be intoxicating. Being surrounded by such intense romance can trick you both into thinking you are falling in love. The reality is that it's the simplest everyday things, such as cooking at home, going for a hike, or checking out a farmers' market, that give you an actual representation of your budding relationship. Dates should consist of activities and experiences to give you and the person you're dating an opportunity to gain a deeper understanding of one another.

I've yet to meet a person who hasn't experienced something they refer to as the worst first date ever. We've all had them! Since I've been back in the dating game, I've learned there are certain rules when dating to avoid an unfortunate situation. I asked my friends from the show if they would share their biggest disaster dates and what they learned from each experience. There's definitely something to take away from each of their stories!

Haley Ferguson, season twenty

I once went hiking on a first date. Mind you, I don't hike or do anything involving dirt, bugs, or the outdoors, for that matter. The thing is, I wanted to impress this really cute guy. By the time we made it close enough to the top of the mountain, I was completely miserable and out of breath. As I was wondering what ailment I'd have to fake in order for search and rescue to fly me home in an air-conditioned chopper, my date started to flirt by tickling me. I tried to get him to stop by squirming away. I missed a step, twisted my ankle, and rolled down the freaking mountain. It turns out that a busted ankle doesn't get you a rescue chopper, by the way. I didn't want to make him feel badly, plus I was still trying to win the hiker's heart, so I played it cool the rest of the way down while secretly dying in agony. The bruises faded, but my distaste for hiking didn't. Since then, I've stayed true to myself when it comes to dates, especially first ones. I'm not afraid to suggest alternative ideas or straight up tell them I'm not scaling a mountain. Not for him, not for anyone.

Danielle Lombard (aka D-Lo), season twenty-one

I love me some technology, but dating apps were never really my thing. To me, dating on an app seems superficial. Judging whether or not I want to go out with someone based on his photos, job description, and favorite song is too surface level. I'd rather know right off the bat: Is there chemistry? Are we able to carry a conversation? But then again, dating in L.A. can be really tough. People rarely commit to a single relationship, because they feel like there's always something better that may come along. After talking to some of my friends who were dating on apps, I figured I didn't have much to lose.

It was hard for me to take it seriously at first, and there are so many profiles to go through. Then I came across this guy's profile and, for whatever reason, it spoke to me. I figured, what the heck. Let's do this. We texted back and forth for a few days and everything was going great. He was witty and good at keeping a conversation going. Seemed fun and outgoing. I was really excited when he asked me out. He even offered to pick me up for the date, which felt chivalrous and sweet.

As soon as he picked me up, I knew it wasn't going to work. The flirtatious and outgoing guy on the phone was actually very shy and introverted in person. Keeping a conversation going was really hard. To make matters worse, our destination was over an hour away! I didn't think things could get worse once we got there, but they did. He said he forgot something in the car and when he returned, he had a giant professional camera. I thought, *This is weird*. I began noticing every time we were apart he would pull up the camera to snap a shot of me. I'd awkwardly walk out of frame, not wanting to be the subject of whatever it was he wanted to shoot. The entire date was a whopping five hours.

Since then, I've set some ground rules for first dates. One, nobody is picking me up. I'm either driving myself or taking an Uber. Two, never again am I committing to a full-day date until we've established a good relationship. Meeting for coffee or a drink is much better because there's an easy out if things aren't going so well. Third, I now casually let my date know I have plans later on. That way, there's an end to a bad date, and if things are going well, I can say my plans got cancelled. Oh, and if he brings out a long-lens camera, run!

Lace Morris, season twenty

The worst date I've ever been on was so bad because it will stay with me forever. I still can't believe I was the girl who got matching tattoos with her boyfriend. I knew I wanted to get a tattoo to commemorate my incredible time at *Paradise*. I was thinking maybe a little palm tree or an island, something cute and tropical. The producers liked my idea and instantly went into production mode. They were like, "Let's do this as a date!" Before I knew it, Grant and I were planning what tattoo we'd get together.

We chose "Grace," a combination of Grant and Lace. As this conversation was happening, I knew it was a bad idea. As I was walking into the tattoo parlor, I said, "This is a very bad idea." After three shots of tequila I thought, *This is not my best idea, but whatever.* Thanks a lot, tequila.

My brain was flooded with thoughts as *grace* was being permanently scribbled into my wrist. I figured this matching tattoo would either be the greatest thing I'd done or the dumbest thing I'd ever do. I even yelled out, "Why are we doing this right now?!" Grant and I were having a great time together on *Paradise* and I did love him. But we've all thought at some point

we were in love with "the one," only to find out later we were wrong about that person. I found out three months later.

After our breakup, Grant had his tattoo covered with a black rose. I decided instead of covering mine up I'd give it a new meaning. Today, when I look at my wrist I think about the word *grace* as in the grace of God. It reminds me of my strength, faith, and blessings. If I could rewind time, would I have not gotten the tattoo? Of course! I regretted it before it even happened. But we live and then we learn—and then we load up on cute stackable bracelets.

Ben Higgins, season twenty

In my freshman year of college, there was a girl I admired from a distance. I'd seen her around campus and was always taken by how absolutely gorgeous she was. I finally approached her in the food court and she agreed to go out with me. I was so excited and wanted this date to go perfectly. After the date, we went back to my dorm room to watch a movie. My roommate and I had a bunk bed. I didn't want to make her hike to

my top bunk so, since he was out, we crashed on my room-mate's lower bunk to watch a movie on the computer. Things were going great. We were cuddling and getting closer. This date was going way better than I imagined. Then suddenly my roommate unexpectedly entered our room. My date and I jumped up, feeling embarrassed for snuggling on his bed. To balance herself, she put her arm down on top of a working humidifier. She got third-degree burns on her hand and up her arm. It was horrible! We never saw each other again, but I'll bet she still has the scars to always remember me.

Jen Saviano, season twenty

One day, when visiting L.A. and out to lunch by myself, I locked eyes with a really good-looking guy. He was looking sharp in a suit and sitting with another guy in a suit. It was clear they were in the middle of a business lunch. After a few shared glances, he came right up to my table. He leaned in very close to my face, almost too close. Go figure I had a mouthful of steak in my face. Skipping any sort of small talk, he got right down to it.

"Can we get coffee one day?" he asked.

I was taken aback by his directness. I'm not used to guys being so forward. I figured, I don't live in L.A. and I don't have many friends here. It might be nice to know someone. Why not?

A few days later I met him for dinner at a restaurant. Although he was very handsome, he was also very weird. It seemed as if he did a ton of research on me before our date. He had a million questions about my being on *The Bachelor*. He also referenced several of my Instagram stories, which made me feel pretty uncomfortable. While we were sitting at the bar, he continued to lean in too close when talking to me. If I can feel your breath on my face, you're way too close! Even the bartender noticed I was continuously leaning back in attempt to gain some space. After dinner, he invited me to come over to his place for a drink, and I agreed. Part of me didn't want to throw in the towel with this really cute, nice enough guy. I wanted to be open-minded. We took his car because he said his place was right around the corner, which it definitely wasn't. When we got to his house, he started getting very touchy-feely with me. I flat-out said no. After a few nos, I even asked him, "Do you know what 'no' means?" At that point I called for an Uber.

This date taught me to always trust my instincts. This guy wasn't taking my cues early on as to how uncomfortable I was with his in-my-face demeanor, but also, maybe I wasn't communicating this clearly enough. The fact he was a bit of a space invader from the moment we met should have been a red flag to me that perhaps I wouldn't be comfortable with his aggressive nature. Today I am much clearer when it comes to my boundaries, and I am much better about listening to my instincts about when to call it a night.

Ashley Iaconetti, season nineteen

I went on three dates with this one guy. I knew he wasn't my person and I wasn't planning to go another date with him, but then on date number three he asked me what I was doing on Valentine's Day. "Galentine's Day party!" didn't come to my mind because I was so put on the spot and I ended up saying, "Um, nothing." So I ended up going on date number four on Valentine's Day, and I *thought* it would be better than sitting at home alone.

He was a nice guy, but not only was there no spark, we had virtually nothing to talk about. I smiled and nodded and said, "Oh" a lot. We went to the one place you can successfully hang out with someone with whom you have nothing to say: the movies.

My date was nice enough to get me a popcorn and soda. When we went to check in, the ticket attendant let us know we could have used our ticket stubs for free popcorn. I thought my date was joking when he asked, "Can I return her popcorn?"

But this guy proceeded to wait in line to get the $4 my popcorn cost back on his credit card. It was so embarrassing. As if that wasn't bad enough, he drank my soda the whole movie without asking. It was the worst Valentine's Day ever.

Advice for all the single ladies: Don't go out with a guy you think is just "meh" on Valentine's Day. You're much better off staying at home alone with chocolate and your poochie.

Emily Ferguson, season twenty

My first date ever was in high school. I went on a double date to the movies with my friend Mace, her boyfriend, and his friend. Halfway through the movie I asked Mace to go to the bathroom with me. As soon as we got out of the theater, I told her, "I just can't do it! He has boogers in his nose and has the worst Dorito breath!" We went back into the theater, and I didn't think I'd ever see my date again. But, surprise, surprise, I ended up dating that guy for five years! From that I learned to always give people a chance. I mean, who hasn't had Dorito breath at some point? Really.

Chapter Eleven

Social Media Butterfly

*A*FTER GETTING BOOTED FROM BEN'S SEASON, I was expecting to go back to my "normal" life. No more on-camera interviews, no more roses, and definitely no more dates. At least for a little while anyway. My job as an esthetician seemed to be waiting for me, and I was looking forward to hanging with my girls every day and settling back into good ol' San Juan Capistrano.

When I first announced that I was a contestant on the show (and of course with my standard *Bachelor* headshot), I noticed that people were starting to follow me on Instagram, scrolling *all* the way back to my very first posts trying to figure out who I was and what "type" of contestant I would be. I went from having roughly 2,000 followers to about 20,000 curious followers who I thought for sure were going to unfollow me when the show was over.

I think Ben's season was really the first time Instagram played a vital part in direction, buzz, and conversation. By the time the show was about to air and contestants were already announced, everyone had already had their favorites based on looks and Instagram personality and knew little bits of details about each and every one of us. It was something we all weren't used to: having the world creep up on you to see if you were going to be the future Mrs. Higgins.

As the show continued to air, and especially after the first episode, I noticed that more and more people were taking interest in my social media. I sort of just ignored it and continued to post what I normally would. Before I was even a contestant on the show, I loved using Instagram as a creative outlet and always posted about fashion or the girls in cute outfits. I really did believe that once the season was over and the world knew I wasn't the winner, no one would be invested in my life. Why should they be? I was no longer vying for Ben's heart and would just go back to living out my life with Kins and Char.

When the cat was finally out of the bag that I was sent home, it was so nice and relieving to be able to join the rest of the world when it came to conversations about *The Bachelor*. I didn't have to worry or feel like I was going to accidentally let something slip in a comment, but things kind of took a turn after the episode where I was sent home aired. Instead of losing followers, my Instagram took the biggest jump since the night the first episode aired: I suddenly went from 20,000 followers to 400,000 followers *literally* overnight. It was such a monumental jump that I had no idea what to do or how to approach it. I actually think my phone died from getting

I love going to iconic places in different cities and sharing
it with you guys on Instagram. It's such a fun way for
me to creatively share where I'm traveling.

too many notifications. I didn't even bother plugging it in to
see where it was all going to go. It was honestly just so overwhelming at first.

Things went from zero to one hundred real quick for me
when it came to social media. I started to get tons of direct

messages, emails to my personal email account, and nonstop comments. Eventually, I felt like I needed help managing this world because there weren't really guidelines out there. Finding an agent wasn't difficult because, well, I didn't really need to look too hard. They were all coming to me. I signed with Paul, my current agent, and he helped tremendously by showing me how to navigate through the new and upcoming "influencer" space. He also took on the role of handling new partnerships and collaborations. Eventually, with my agent's help, I was able to get a grasp on how to handle the size of my new audience and wrap my head around the newfound value of my social media presence.

Once it clicked with me that social media and "influencing" (so to speak) could truly be a career path, I started to take things seriously. Maybe even too seriously. For a little while, I have to admit I was in a really low place, especially after my first time on *Bachelor in Paradise*. There were nights after I put the girls to sleep where I would nitpick at every little part of my body, from my nose (I really hate my nose) to the missing patch of hair on my brow and how much belly fat I was carrying. I had a totally distorted image of myself because I was invested in the comments that people would leave on social media. The things that people say are not secret or inaccessible. I've gotten comments about how my body looked like a twelve-year-old girl's body or how I should "eat a sandwich" because I looked frail and unhealthy. Or that being "that skinny" was not normal and I must be anorexic or sick. The jokes and commentary were so frequent that I let them control my life. Everything

I posted resulted in my obsession with what strangers on the internet were saying, and Facetune (an airbrushing and photo-editing app) turned into my best friend. I look back on my photos now and can admit that I over-airbrushed a lot of my photos because of my own insecurity. I let others' opinions dictate how I felt about the way I looked. It went really downhill when people started to say things about Kins and Char.

Before I was big on Instagram, I used to follow the accounts of many other moms and single moms. I loved that there was a community of women I could look up to and relate to. I didn't feel so alone. I wanted to use my platform as a pillar for other single moms going through the same thing and have always posted pictures of the girls, whether they were candid or styled. When my numbers grew, I just wanted to stay true to what I've always done on social media—up until I got scathing comments like how I put my daughters in the wrong car seats or how dairy was bad for them and I shouldn't allow them to eat pizza. Or how I was overexposing them by dressing them in two-piece bikinis on the beach rather than one-piece swimsuits.

Once I posted what I thought was a sweet photo of Kinsley and me kissing, and I got a ton of backlash on it. People were saying it was grossly inappropriate for me to kiss my daughter on the lips and that she shouldn't be kissing any girls. If I posted too much of the girls, I would get comments about how I'm just using my own children to gain "likes" and publicity, and if I didn't post them, I would get questions about where they were and why I was "never with them." Of course, my

These are the photos that caused an uproar on social media and made me realize how Instagram sometimes has no boundaries.

favorite comments are those that call me a bad mom and say I should stop "making out with guys on TV" and "go be a parent instead." I can't even begin to explain how many times I had to answer the question, "Where are your kids?" when I was out with my girlfriends or out of town.

People expect answers when you let them into your life via social media, but what they don't realize is that every minute of your life is not blasted on the internet. Co-parenting was a difficult subject for people to grasp and people also seemed to forget that sometimes grandparents come to the rescue when you need a last-minute sitter. It seemed like everything about my life was a topic of discussion, with no escape from the negativity. To this day, there are some comments that still haunt me, but not ones about myself. The ones that have been the most hurtful are comments about how Kinsley or Charlie *look*. It is like having a knot in my stomach when I have to read those comments, and it honestly makes me so nervous to think about what they are going to have to go through when growing up with social media.

Of course, everything always seems perfect on social media, but I never showed how much these small comments really affected me. Maybe people thought I wouldn't see them, or it was okay because they weren't saying it directly to my face. Regardless, it took me at least a year to begin braving through my insecurity. Every photo I debated about posting, examining it with eagle eyes and always having another set of eyes look at it before I shared it. Slowly but surely, I began to let the weight lift a little off my shoulders, and I started to be less and less self-conscious about what people were going to say.

At the end of the day, my face is going to be my face, my body is going to be my body, and I'm always going to try to be the best mom I can ever be. I love my girls and have raised them for years on my own. It took me a long time to find the courage to ask for help when it came to raising them, and I finally let myself off the hook for needing help from my mom or from my family. Kins and Char are perfect in my eyes, and no one could ever change my mind about that. Once I started to break free from the toxic comments on social media, I started to be more and more comfortable with just focusing on the community of women I have online who have done nothing but encourage me. It's really easy to get wrapped up in all the negativity, but I have to say I am so grateful for the women who come to my defense online time and time again. I finally realized that's where I would prefer my energy to go, and I would much rather be grateful for girls who have my back than focus on people who are quick to judge and say hateful things behind a keyboard.

Nowadays, the number one rule I follow is to never read the comments, especially during times when sh*t hits the fan and bad publicity gets circulated. Some of you may remember a few times when the media spun stories out of control in regards to what was going on in my life. At first, I was glued to my phone every minute of every hour of every day reading comments and all the latest articles to hit the web. Once I started to take social media a little less seriously and stopped caring what people were saying, I felt more at peace. I no longer had to question my own integrity just because someone I didn't know was saying something negative about me.

Overall, social media has taught me a whirlwind of things, but one thing I always live by is to be authentic to my audience. I remain as transparent as possible, with careful regard to what I keep private. I realize that, as a public figure, I *am* somewhat obligated to be a role model and to set an example. I do acknowledge and notice that I have a lot of young female followers, and, having two girls myself, I always keep in mind what my actions or words could possibly teach or portray. I love being able to use my platform for good, and the values that I showcase online are not different from who I am offline. It's always so funny when I meet someone in person and they tell me, "Oh! You actually are nice! And normal." I can't tell you how big of a shock it is for me when someone online is totally different from who they are offline! It's a good reminder for me to always remember that nobody's life is perfect, and that what I value is being authentic no matter where I go—whether it's online or offline.

Speaking of on- and offline personalities, one of the biggest things that changed for me after growing on social media was my dating life. I mean, my dating life changed a lot in general after being on the show, and I sincerely thought being on *The Bachelor* would be the most unique dating experience I had, but it definitely escalated from there. Things "going down in the DM" was an actual real-life thing and not just a Yo Gotti song. Before I became extremely cautious about who I would respond to in my direct messages, I took a few chances on guys who would private message me and ask me out on a date. Don't worry—of course it was always agreed upon to meet in a well-lit, public place with lots of people around. Nothing serious came from any of my conversations in my DMs (until Bobby came around), but one of the funniest stories I have to share had to do with a guy who was *so* interested in *The Bachelor* and in Bachelor Nation that he spent the whole night asking me about what the show was like, what Chris Harrison was "really like in real life," and so on. He didn't have a single question for me about my real life. Some people think that a lot of guys are interested in me because of the following I have on social media, but, most of the time, guys are actually really turned off or intimidated by it.

A lot of my dating life is portrayed (and often misinterpreted) in the media, but—surprise!—there *are* guys with whom I've gone on multiple dates who have never appeared in the press or social media. In any case, whether you're an influencer or not, posting a guy on your social media is a huge deal. It makes things so much more official and real. Almost as real as the ranking of your Top 8 on Myspace. When I first started dating Bobby, I was reluctant to post him on social media. From the beginning, he was the sweetest, chillest guy I have ever dated. After a few months of growing our relationship, he posted a picture of me on his Instagram and I kind of, sort of, freaked out. Having him post me on his social media meant that he was acknowledging our relationship for the whole world to see (to be dramatic), and as much as I didn't want to hide him, I was really nervous to see how people would react when I finally introduced him on my page.

Initially, one of the reasons I didn't want to post about Bobby is because he is seriously the nicest, most considerate man I have ever been with. I really would have hated for him to receive any negative comments or backlash. Without intentionally doing so, though, I did sort of make him feel as if I was hiding him because it took me so long to be comfortable posting about him. He was never truly angry or upset, and he understood where I was coming from with my reluctance to post, but it was a serious conversation we had to have when it came to my social media presence. My anxiety about posting him on my Instagram was something that I had to get over.

Nothing but big smiles in this photo, but it wasn't
always easy to share about our relationship.

People truly are so invested in my love life that I was afraid
of getting publicly burned . . . again. In the end, I let all the bad
thoughts slide. Even if I can't picture us breaking up anytime
soon, I have to tell myself that life is life and things happen.
Relationships come and go until you find the right one, and I

can't live in fear of what could possibly happen and hold back. I just have to live my life.

One of the reasons I wanted to dedicate a whole chapter to social media and the influencer world is because I realize there is such a major interest in it. I get many direct messages and emails asking for advice on how to get started or if I can provide any tips or tricks that helped me grow my own social media. To be fair, and before heading into the rest of this chapter, I want to throw out a disclaimer that, while I may seem like an expert, social media honestly wasn't something I ever envisioned myself getting into or using as a career. I am so very thankful every day that I get to create and showcase my highlight reel (and sometimes very real moments) within such a powerful community, but, at the end of the day, I am just trying my best. I've learned over time that just because a post doesn't perform as well as I expected it to or if I regret something I posted and it was too late to delete or archive it, I just kind of roll with the punches. I also have to 100 percent acknowledge that Bachelor Nation most definitely helped skyrocket my numbers, and that it's far from ordinary to go from a couple of thousand followers to nearly 400,000 overnight. My experience with social media fame is definitely unique compared to what the "normal" route to becoming big on social media is (if there even is a normal way).

I think most people go into the idea of becoming a social media influencer under the pretense that if you just share your passions and be your true, authentic self (which is so, so important), your numbers will just organically grow, and you'll get tons of offers for sponsored posts. I think what most influencers don't really talk too much about, though, is that the game of numbers can really get to your head—almost to a point where you feel like you're failing and that people aren't enjoying your content, and therefore, they are rejecting you. I cannot stress enough how much I have to detox myself from this thinking or how long it took me to get out of my own head. If you're scared to put yourself out there for fear of rejection, surround yourself with the most supportive friends and family who will encourage you to get your creativity out in the world. Even though I've reached more than a million followers (which still shocks me nearly every day!), I still need my hype-women surrounding me who all encourage and give me words of affirmation. Know that you're not alone if you're afraid of jumping into a new career path, and if this is something you want to do, you should just get out there and do it!

A lot of people ask me what being sponsored for a post really looks like and how much I get paid or compensated for a post. I've tried to get a definitive method for what I should charge or aim to make when it comes to posts by having multiple conversations with friends who are also in the space, but we almost always end up having completely different experiences or answers. Because of our differentiating numbers, engagement, location, and connection to the brand, there really is no cookie-cutter answer.

Brand marketing, which has turned into its own beast with influencer marketing or social media marketing, is multifaceted and is constantly changing. The rapidly changing and saturated market makes it incredibly difficult to put this industry into a box. Like other careers, there are systems in place and an overall ballpark for numbers. Nothing about the influencer industry is guaranteed or set in stone. In just a couple of years, I've heard all terms, from "blogger" to all varieties of "influencer": macro influencer, micro influencer, mini influencer, beauty influencer, fashion influencer, lifestyle influencer, and so on and so forth. The list is endless and a bit overwhelming. I do know, however, that many of my followers (for whom I'm so, so thankful) are interested in entering the space on their own career paths. For the rest of this chapter, I'll try my best to provide insightful information that will break down my experiences, failures, fears, and successes when it came to building and managing my social media channels.

Overall, social media is a tricky, messy, and overwhelming yet fun field. Every day, I am discovering new things that work for me and realizing things that used to work for me all of a sudden don't. My followers are also growing with me, so new interests come about and new, fresh content needs to come out too. If you were to ask me where I think my career will be in ten years, I wouldn't know what to tell you. I wouldn't even know what to say if you asked me where my career will be in two or three years. What I hope you pull away from this chapter are some practical tips that will help you navigate through your career, whether your goal or dream is to be an influencer or whether you're a small brand trying to play in the big, bad world of influencer marketing. Most importantly of all, though, I hope that after reading this chapter, you'll see that social media, although a positive tool in our world, is not as important as enjoying the moments that you get to live out in real life.

All right. Here goes nothing!

Garnering a price for your social media value, like I mentioned before, is the toughest issue for me to tackle. Realistically, in a traditional work setting, it is definitely frowned upon to turn to your coworker on your team and ask them to disclose their current salary and benefits. It's exactly how I feel when someone asks me how much I generally make for a sponsored post, especially if they're not asking from a business standpoint. Of course, you'd share your salary with discretion and only to your most trusted, inner circle, but I've been in too many conversations in which numbers were thrown around loosely and feelings were inevitably hurt. With all that being said, I won't be sharing my current rate per post in this chapter, but I would say that engagement (how many people interact on your page and how invested people are in responding to your content) is much more important than the number of followers you have.

For a practical way to understand numbers, there are endless articles out there explaining how you can calculate your engagement. On average, anything above a 1 percent engagement on Instagram is a solid number for you to try to build up to. The higher the number of followers you have, though, the harder it is to achieve a decent engagement. Someone with 500 followers likely has actual, personal relationships with all those people, and therefore those followers will like and comment on their pics. Whereas someone with 50,000 followers—well, nobody knows that many people! The followers act more like bystanders and tend to engage less often on the posts. So a good rule of thumb for engagement is if you have 10,000 followers, your engagement should be around 5 to 6 percent as a healthy medium. If you're at 1 million followers, anything above 1 percent is really good. If you're in the middle, around 200,000 to 400,000 followers, your engagement should be around 2 to 4 percent. Once you understand your engagement percentage, you can use that number to leverage with brands to work out a deal.

I am so fortunate to have a team behind me, from my agency, Central Entertainment Group (CEG), to a brand manager and assistant, who all help negotiate numbers for me, but keep in mind that all of your talent and hard work most definitely deserve more than just product trade or commission. When I first started growing on social media after the show, I got tons and tons of direct messages from brands asking me if they could send me product of their newest line or things that they thought the girls and I would like. Being so new and fresh at the time, I agreed and thought I was just receiving gifts. Months later, though, when I never posted or mentioned them (for reasons such as the clothes not fitting properly or just my forgetfulness . . . oops), the brands would send me angry emails or direct messages asking me why I haven't posted for them. I quickly learned that I always needed to be clear that if they were just wanting to send me PR (public relations) packages or gifts, I would not be able to guarantee a post or mention on my social media. If they did want to work out a campaign or sponsored post with me, I made sure to clearly lay out the guidelines of what I needed to post, the timeline, and of course, what budget the brand was working with. Here's a template of a letter used by my brand manager in response to first-time inquiries about gifting:

Hi [Name],

Thank you so much for reaching out to Amanda. She is so grateful that you're interested in gifting her.

Before sending over the right address, we wanted to make sure that we are all on the same page. Unfortunately, for gifting and product-trade only, Amanda won't be able to guarantee a post. However, if she does post on her social media with your products, she will most likely tag the brand or answer any questions of where the product came from.

Let us know if you're still interested, and if so, would love to send over her address.

Thank you!

That said, I've done many Instagram campaigns for a tenth of my average rate just because I fell in love with the brand or have been a loyal fan for a long time. Not every influencer is so open to posting about a product without a fee. For me, it's a case-by-case basis and all about being comfortable with what I'm doing. If you're the owner of a brand aspiring to work with influencers, just believe in your product and the right influencers will come along who align with your budget and your brand.

Also remember that not all sponsored posts work the same. I usually offer tiers or packages to my posts. Some brands also just prefer Instagram stories, or a Facebook live post, or static posts (posts that are on your feed). Some brands want to add in a trackable link, discount code, or a "Swipe Up to Shop" call to action. Right at this second as I'm writing this chapter, the value of an Instagram story is a bit more than the value of a static or Instagram feed post. This can totally change by tomorrow—who knows? What I do know and suggest is that creating different price points to give to brands will help you secure a sponsored post. Having three different price points and creating hard rules about what content you can and cannot provide will save you a lot of time and push and pull.

It also helped me a lot to understand my market as a mom with two sweet girls. With the power of social media and entrepreneurship, there are so many creative people and brands out there who now have a platform to share their work, value, and ideas. What solidifies my place in the space is that I can share my work experiences with Kinsley and Charlie, who were only two and four when my Instagram started picking up momentum. I don't necessarily like to stick myself in only a mommy-and-me category, but I love being able to involve the girls in my work. I do sometimes wonder when I'll let them take control of their own social media, but that is a question I have yet to answer. For now, I love that they enjoy having fun and playing with the newest children's brands and clothes.

Charlie now wants to do my makeup, and Kinsley was on a glitter-dresses-only bender for a *looong* time just from being sent a sparkly dress one time. So really, like mother, like daughters, I guess!

I don't know when I'll retire the mommy and me outfits.
I guess when they're old enough to tell me no.

Understanding your community and who you specifically want to reach can help you understand what direction you'd like to go with your social media. I mentioned briefly before that I was always sharing about fashion on my channel, and I am seriously the girliest girly girl, so any chance to share about beauty is something that I love, too. Fashion, kids' style, and beauty are things that just make sense to me, almost as if they were ingrained in my DNA ever since I was little. Because they come naturally to me, I knew they were the best things to continue sharing on my social media after the show. Tap into what comes naturally to you and what you have the most expertise in because that's what's going to be the most authentic and the easiest content for you to create. People will always be able to tell when you're being genuine or not, so remember to keep that in mind.

Many times, I look at other bloggers and influencers and love their content. We're all guilty of wanting to model our page or Instagram after another person, and sometimes, I ask myself how I can curate content like another blogger. What I constantly have to remind myself, though, is that's just not me. And as much as I would love to take a beautiful flatlay, I'm actually kind of terrible at them. The word "curated" gets thrown out a lot when it comes to social media, but, honestly, there's not really a formula I go by. Artistically, I like to make sure I take the best-quality photos with my favorite edits (in which I don't claim to be an expert), but I don't implement a posting schedule or a social media planner to lay out my grid. There is a consistency with everything, but planning my grid doesn't take over my life. My day to day is already crazy enough, and I share so much on a whim that sharing content on the spot is now just a part of me and my branding. Bottom line is this: You have to do what works for you, and if you're all about your aesthetic appearance on your feed and Instagram story, that's what you should do.

Another reason why you should carefully choose how to reach your audience is because your workload only gets bigger and bigger when it becomes a passion of yours. With work being social media and social media being work, work is never-ending. There is no start and stop time, no time for you to clock in and out. However, the ability to have a flexible schedule is one of the reasons why I am so grateful for my career in social media. I can't help but laugh at the common misconception that working in social media is nothing but taking pictures in pretty places. It is such a creative field where you're not only in charge of what content you push or the copy you write but also in charge of the finance and business aspect of it. I was running this as a one-woman show for the longest time until I finally caved in and hired an assistant.

Pushing out your life online every day seems like a fun thing to do (and it really is!), but there is a demand there that no one really addresses. Sometimes, there are days when I just want to go offline, but I notice that even on the days when I'm absent on social media or when I'm not posting for a few days, I actually lose followers. Don't get me wrong—you *really* can't let yourself get wrapped up too much in the toxicity of who's following you and who's not. It's definitely something that I've been mindful not to become obsessed with, but as in any self-owned business, you have to pay attention to the numbers, even if just a little bit. When this happens to me, I don't panic; I tell myself that social media is constantly changing. In my opinion, it is definitely here to stay. If you're totally and completely fearless about starting this journey, you'll gain a huge chunk of knowledge about yourself and who you are as a creator. Not to mention you'll also gain a ton of business experience, which can only be a win-win for yourself.

If I were to leave you with one last piece of advice, it would be to never take yourself too seriously. I spent way too long worrying about and obsessing over things that mattered a lot in the digital world but not so much in the real world. Be sure of yourself, your values, and who you are, and always surround yourself with a group of people *offline* who will be honest and real with you.

Chapter Twelve

Girl Code

I THINK AT EVERY POINT of a girl-mom's life, you think about what your daughter will have to endure when she hits junior high or high school. Maybe I grew up in a unicorn home or in a family that was sprinkled in fairy dust, but Carissa and I never really fought *that* much. We had normal bickering sessions, but, all in all, we've always had each other's backs. It was a shock to my system when I entered adolescence only to realize not all relationships with girls were like that of mine with my sister. Quickly I learned about the gossip and the boy drama, the back stabbing and the lies. Being a teenager is no joke. I think society often pits girls against each other, and we're sometimes put into situations where we're meant to tear each other down. But there's nothing better than being a true girls' girl.

High school nowadays seems like even more of a danger zone—I mean, more so than what it was like when I was in

Couldn't imagine a life without a baby sis (who really acts like my older sis sometimes). I could cry thinking about how proud I am of her!

there a billion years ago. Now, kids have social media, which is one thing that I never had to deal with back then. If there were mean girls at school, the drama stayed at school. Now, who knows what will slide into Kins's and Char's DMs one day when I finally let them on social media . . . am I right?

Chances are the girls aren't going to tell me everything that goes on in their lives, no matter how cool a mom I strive to be. If they take one piece of advice from me to prepare for this girl world, I hope it will be to build their tribe. Whether you're six, sixteen, or sixty, you lean on your sisterhood of friends to get through pretty much anything. Even as an adult when I'm bullied on social media, I get through it by turning to my tribe, who are always there to remind me it's all good. I hope my daughters see firsthand how important my friendships are and build strong, supportive tribes of their own. That's why I think it's so important they—and we— understand the importance of GIRL CODE.

Writing this list of girl codes that I've learned over the years is my reminder to all girls and women that we've got to stick together.

GIRL CODE #1: Don't Get So Wrapped Up in a Relationship You Take Your Girlfriends for Granted.

I was once in a relationship with a guy who was pretty controlling. This guy, let's just call him Josh, wanted my attention at all times and didn't like me hanging out with my girlfriends. Girls' nights were completely out of the question. He didn't even like me grabbing a quick lunch with my friends. I quickly became that flaky friend. I was bailing on birthday dinners and taking a week to respond in our group chats, and I just wasn't being the good friend I'd always considered myself to be. My friends were definitely hurt that I was blowing them off and frustrated with my behavior. As soon as Josh and I broke up, I needed my friends to be there for me, but I felt so horrible turning to them after neglecting them for so long. Luckily, I have an amazing group of friends who understood and forgave me. From this experience I learned to never let any romantic relationship compromise the important ones I have with my friends. Friendships are relationships too, and any guy you're dating, engaged to, or married to should respect that and allow you to nurture your relationships with the people that are close to you.

GIRL CODE #2: Always Ask Your Girlfriends How They're Doing. And Mean It.

In this digital age, it's easy to just send random texts to friends for a quick check-in. What's up? How's it goin'? A fast touch-base to say, "Hi, I'm thinking of you." But is that really enough? I don't think so. Make the time to really connect, whether it's a phone call or a deeper text that actually allows room for your friends to open up about anything that they're going through. This is a quality I value so much in my inner circle. We have a priceless group chat that's always going off with funny memes, inside jokes, or screenshots from guys we are texting with, but often we give each other a solo check-in on the side to see how we're really doing. When someone does this for me, it means the world.

GIRL CODE #3: Be Prepared to Swing by with Snacks, Wine, and Tissues at Any Given Time.

Life's hardest moments are a tricky thing, but they can be conquered when your closest girlfriends are around. Sometimes, you don't even have to say anything or have any words prepared. Just the action of showing up, zero questions asked, is the most memorable thing that you could do.

When I was going through a really awful breakup, I wanted to just be left alone. I wasn't in the mood to go out or even pull myself together enough to be in public. Three of my friends decided to get together and surprise me at my apartment. They brought wine and we talked for hours—okay, let's be real, I ugly-cried for hours. Once the sob-fest was over, they pulled me out of my funk and a dance party to Bruno Mars on my kitchen counter ensued until 2 AM. And it honestly made me feel better! Sometimes your friends know what you need more than you do, and having friends who are there for you during dark times is so important.

GIRL CODE #4: Have Extra Pasties on You. And Tampons. And Hair Ties. And Bobby Pins. Hand It Off to Any Girl You Meet in the Bathroom Who May Be in Need.

This is a tribute to all the girls who have saved me when I was in need. Thank you—you know who you are.

It's so important to be able to lean on a group of
strong and trusted women. My aunt Traciee and
cousin Elle are part of that core group for me.

GIRL CODE #5: Don't Hate. Appreciate.

I'm sure everyone has had a moment when you've felt ridic-
ulously undermined by another girl in the room. She's crazy
gorgeous, she's sweet, and, basically, she makes you feel like

you spent two hours getting ready to look like the Pinterest fail version of her.

It's in this very moment when you get to decide what kind of girl you want to be: one who looks for the flaws and fumes over this girl's greatness, or one who appreciates the beautiful creature she is. I've always come from a place of celebrating instead of hating. I'll often genuinely compliment ladies rather than keep my admiration to myself. Why wouldn't I? The girl world needs more kindness and compliments and less envy and cattiness.

GIRL CODE #6: When It Comes to Dating from Your Friend's Inner Circle, Knock Before Entering.

Sometimes it seems like my dating pool is the same size as a kiddie pool. Whether it's in the town we live in or within Bachelor Nation, somehow everyone is connected in some way. It's inevitable you'll encounter a guy you want to date and then find out, go figure, he is connected to one of your friends. It's been a common situation for me to be interested in getting to know someone who has dated one of my friends. I've always thought being open and honest with all parties involved is the best and only policy here.

One of my close girlfriends went on a couple dates with this really cute hockey player. He was a single dad. She was really into him and even told me all about him, glowing over how excited she was. After the third date, they realized they were too different from one another and never pursued each other again. Actually, she met another guy a few days later and they're now engaged! Well, the cute hockey player slid into my DMs shortly after their engagement. He was very respectful and told me how happy he was for her and then asked if it would be weird if he asked me out. I was definitely interested. He was cute and a single dad. But I didn't want to hurt my friend or step on any toes. I dug up the courage to call my friend and tell her about the messages, asking if she would mind if I went out with him. After all, she was happily engaged now and only went on a couple dates with this guy. But you never know how someone might respond. She did think it was a little odd I was essentially stepping into her place but eventually gave me the green light to go out with him. Spoiler alert: We texted for about a month and never even ended up going out. Regardless, I'm glad I checked with her first because continuing on without her knowing would have been wrong.

Keeping secrets or going behind a friend's back is never okay. And while it might be an awkward conversation, it will make things a lot easier in the long run. And if a friend tells you she's not comfortable with it, I say you should respect that. As long as it's within reason: If your friend went on a single date with a guy six years ago and you think he might be your soul mate, yet she forbids it . . . then that's a different case. But I would always put yourself in their shoes and handle it in the way you would want it to be handled if the roles were reversed.

GIRL CODE #7: Don't Flirt, Pursue, or Date a Guy If You Know That He Is Still Working Things Out with His Almost-But-Not-Quite-Ex-Girlfriend.

If you watched season four of *Bachelor in Paradise*, you were dragged along with the rest of us through the love triangle between Dean, Kristina, and D-Lo. If you missed this one, Dean Unglert and Kristina Schulman were a seemingly strong couple up until he came across the sparkly new arrival, Danielle Lombard, aka D-Lo.

D-Lo was really into Dean—I mean, how could you not be? And she didn't see anything wrong with pursuing someone who was interested in her, too. That is, after all, the name of the game in *Paradise*. So, Dean broke Kristina's heart by giving his to D-Lo instead. It was incredibly sad to witness firsthand. Kristina really did believe in her relationship with Dean and she had good reason to. He was not being completely forthcoming about his intentions with her. Dean is a good guy, but he didn't know how to handle this situation. He was telling both girls different things, which is usually the case with a guy who is still talking to or dealing with his ex.

When all was said and done, neither relationship lasted. Danielle might have met someone who was emotionally available and ready for commitment had she set her eye on someone who didn't have one foot in the door of his previous relationship. It's a great lesson for us all: Avoid love triangles at all costs. If he has strings attached to someone else, don't get tangled up!

GIRL CODE #8: Never, Ever Body Shame.

After *The Bachelor* aired and I unintentionally blew up on social media, I was blown away by how comfortable other women were putting down my physical appearance. With all the positive attention of being a public figure came equal amounts of negative. I've heard and read the worst of the worst when it comes to my face, body, outfits, hair, personality, and voice. No matter how thick my skin gets over time, it always hurts to some degree.

Since when did this become acceptable behavior? Why do some people feel it's okay to pick others apart on social media? We've all seen it go down in the comments. A special shout-out to those who come to my defense: I appreciate you. In my opinion, girls should never, ever put down each other's appearance. Let's use our words—voices, comments, tweets—to create positive change and affect others by lifting them up!

GIRL CODE #9: Don't Tell Your Friends' Secrets.

As girls, we love to open up and tell each other everything. When you're in a relationship you also want to tell your boyfriend everything. But I've learned it's so important to keep those relationships separate and respect your friend's privacy. I learned this one the hard way. There was a time my friend confided in me she had cheated on her boyfriend. I am so against cheating and I let her know I was very upset with her. Despite my promise not to tell a soul, I confided in my then-boyfriend

Every day I am thankful for the community of women and girls I've met who've uplifted me and have had such a positive influence on my life.

about how upset I was with my friend's choices. I didn't think it counted as a betrayal of trust because I was putting my trust into a person with whom I was supposed to share everything. Well, a few months later this guy and I were in the midst of a nasty breakup. He was angry with me, so much so he threatened to expose my friend just to hurt me. This, of course, frightened and devastated me. The last thing I wanted to do was hurt my friend and affect her relationship.

I'll never forget the desperate fear I carried around hoping he wouldn't say a word. From then on, I vowed to myself that when my friends tell me a secret, I won't tell my boyfriend, my mom—nobody. Not even those I trust the most. I want to be a safe place for my friends and their privacy. Regardless of how small or big the secret may be, keep it between you and your friend! Always.

GIRL CODE #10: If You Know Someone's Boyfriend Is Cheating, Let Her Know. If You're 100 Percent Sure Your Friend Is Being Betrayed, Tell Her What's Up. It's Girl Code.

After I broke up with my ex-husband, I had numerous girl-friends tell me they had seen him on dating apps while we were married. Even my best friend's little sister! I was so upset they didn't tell me sooner. I was completely blindsided when I discovered the truth. It still would have been difficult to hear it from a friend or acquaintance, but I would have found out far sooner than I did. Because of my experience, if I ever were to hear about or see someone's boyfriend cheating, I'd give her a heads-up.

A perfect case in point would be a time when Robby Hayes and I were giving dating another try (I know, I *know*). One night he said he was staying in when—lo and behold—his phone happened to die, making him unreachable. Unfortunately for him a fan of the show saw him making out with a girl that night at a country music concert. This awesome girls' girl caught him mid make-out, snapped photos, and sent them to me on Instagram! I was so glad and super appreciative she did that for me so I didn't waste another second with him. Girls like her who look out for other girls are the real MVPs.

Chapter Thirteen

Now Accepting Me

*I*T'S SAFE TO SAY the last few years have been somewhat of a whirlwind for me. I get asked all the time how I stay optimistic about dating and finding someone after quite a few failed relationships. The truth is, relationships don't always work out. That's kind of the point of dating. That doesn't mean you give up. With every relationship that hasn't worked out for me, I have learned so much about myself, what I want in a partner, and even more so what I *don't* want in a partner. I've also learned quite a bit about my own faults.

My failed relationships have taught me how important it is to be independent and happy on your own. As soon as you're truly content on your own, that's probably when you're going to meet the right guy. Or at least the right guy for now, because note to self: This one may not work out either and that's okay!

It had been months since I went on a date. I was solely focusing on my kids, my career, writing this book, and starting a clothing line. After four years of bad relationships and even worse breakups, getting into a new one was the last thing on my mind. I was flying home from New York City with my assistant Tiffany in January 2018 when I noticed a guy had sent me a message on Instagram—an adorable video of a puppy. I clicked on his profile and looked through his photos and thought he was so cute. A year earlier I would have responded so quickly to his direct message, but after everything I've been through, I decided to ignore it.

A couple of weeks later, he sent me another message and then another, and finally I responded. We exchanged numbers and texted for a couple of weeks. He asked me out on Valentine's Day and at first I thought about getting a babysitter and going on the date but instead decided to stay home with the kids to have our own Valentine's Day celebration. Bobby and I rescheduled for a few days later. I bailed. A few days after ditching this poor guy, my two engaged friends and I had tickets to a Cirque du Soleil show and I needed a date. I decided to ask Bobby. I was still a little skeptical of meeting up with a stranger, so I figured a double date would be perfect. I may or may not have told him it was a double date—my bad. He got in the Uber and was a little surprised to see my two friends sitting in the back seat with me. (I still haven't lived that one down!)

During this date, I was so pleasantly surprised. I wasn't expecting to like this guy at all. I wasn't even in a place where I cared to be in a relationship whatsoever. He was surprisingly super shy for a guy who persistently slid into my DMs. He was sweet and respectful and didn't mention *The Bachelor* or *Bachelor in Paradise* once (he has actually never even seen either of them). Not to mention, he was much more handsome in person. I had a good feeling about him. We said goodbye that night and mentioned we'd see each other soon. We continued to text every day but didn't see each other for nearly three weeks.

Once we started going on actual dates, it took six of them before he kissed me. If you've watched my "love stories" on *Bachelor in Paradise*, you know this is a very different speed for me. But it was so refreshing! We really got to know each other and enjoyed each other's company before getting physical. It wasn't the kind of lustful romance you see in the movies. And honestly, I've had that and it doesn't always work. Just because you have physical chemistry with a guy doesn't mean you're falling in love or that you're compatible in a relationship. Bobby taught me that the most important aspects of a relationship are a lot deeper than having a strong physical chemistry with someone. Because if you're not compatible and that's all you have, you're going to face some serious issues later when things start getting more serious and you start butting heads.

Bobby was a homebody just like me. Finally, a guy who didn't have to see and be seen! Turns out they do exist. I get tired at 10 PM and love staying home in my pajamas with my kids, watching TV. It's harder than I ever imagined to find a guy who doesn't love to party. Before, I wished to find a guy who wanted to live a low-profile life at home, but I figured he wasn't out there and so I settled for compromising with partiers. But Bobby also didn't drink. He didn't order an alcoholic drink on any one of our dates, and I really liked that about him. He was very calm and low key, even slightly introverted. Night and day compared to any guy I'd dated in the past.

Our relationship was different from anything I'd ever experienced before. We were truly best friends. We had each other's backs. We communicated our wants and needs and were on the same page that our relationship was a constant work in progress. He was so great and hands-on with Kinsley and Charlie, but it took a while to build that relationship. I used to have the unrealistic expectation that a guy I was dating needed to love my kids from day one. They're my entire world, of course, but I'm their mother. A new boyfriend understandably has no connection to them. Whomever you're with should slowly build a relationship with your kids, just as a relationship with you was slowly built. My ex Josh claimed to "love" my kids before he even met them. It made my heart melt at the time. But looking back, it was totally a load of crap. I remember the first time Bobby said he loved Kins and Char. It was so much more meaningful because he had actually built a relationship with them and meant it.

At the time, everything was really falling into place, and I had truly never been happier. I was finally in a relationship where I felt like my boyfriend really knew me and loved me. Another new thing for me was the fact that my friends and family all approved of him, which had never happened in my life. After seven months of dating, Bobby and I had dealt with our fair share of arguments—it's only natural. But we had gotten pretty good at knowing what set each other off, what buttons not to push, and how to deal with each other when one of us was frustrated, hurt, or angry. In my past relationships, my buttons were constantly pushed on purpose. With Bobby, I understood what it was like to be with someone who wouldn't do that to me intentionally. We genuinely cared about each other's feelings and wanted to make each other happy. No relationship is perfect, but ours was the closest I've been to finding an authentic relationship that was built slowly and organically. Even though it didn't work out in the end, we could both walk away with key lessons. Bobby and I separated on nothing but good terms, and it makes me happy to know that mature breakups *are* actually possible.

Even in relationships with the smoothest of sailing, you'll face a few swells. For us, the roughest waters happened to occur in a desert—go figure! You may have heard about my incident in September 2018 resulting in a mug shot. Me! A mug shot! I still can't believe it. One of my good friends was having her bachelorette party and never did I think it would be anything other than celebrating her road into marriage.

So, if it was a bachelorette party with just the girls, how did Bobby wind up in Vegas with me? A few weeks prior to the trip, Bobby lost a volleyball tournament he was training really hard for. I'm talking 5 AM wake-up calls every day to practice. He was pretty devastated about it, so I wanted to do something special to cheer him up. His dream was to race a Lamborghini (men . . . amiright?), so I found a place in Vegas that allowed you to race luxury cars. Since I already had plans to be in Vegas, I thought it was the perfect opportunity for me to stay a few days extra and have Bobby meet with me toward the end of the bachelorette party. Obviously, things didn't exactly go as planned, and we never made it out to the racetrack.

Saturday and Sunday were reserved for all things bachelorette. I'm talking day clubs with The Chainsmokers performing and the girls having a good time. The last thing on the weekend's agenda was going to Magic Mike Live on Sunday night. Bobby arrived at the hotel just a few minutes before we were leaving for the show. I quickly said hi, gave him a kiss, and told him I'd come to his room when I got back.

When we got to Magic Mike, I remember all of us grabbing a drink at the bar and finding our seats. I had my bride-to-be friend decked out in all white, hoping the performers would bring her up on stage—and they did! The show was so much fun. As soon as it was over, we were all laughing at my friend's shocked face when she was pulled up on stage.

As the bachelorette party was coming to a close, we opted to end the weekend in the hotel room so that we wouldn't have to walk out and about the strip in heels. Seemed like a pretty good choice all around. We'd be able to avoid club lines, be safe, and not spend a ridiculous amount of money on bottle service or drinks from the bar.

With Bobby there and a group of my closest friends, I allowed myself a night off. We weren't in public and we weren't planning on driving or going anywhere. I felt that I was in a safe place, and to be honest, I never let loose. But that night I had a couple more drinks than usual (and by that, I mean two more than my one normal glass of wine), and we were all kind of being loud in the hotel room. We were there to celebrate, but *never* did we mean to cause a huge disturbance.

With the noise we were making, our neighbors called hotel security, who came to our room. Bobby, who rarely, rarely drank, opened the door to speak to them and apologize on our behalf for being so loud. I don't know what got into me, but I suppose liquid courage happens to the best of us in the worst moments sometimes. I barged up to the door and "pushed" Bobby aside to get in front of him to speak to security myself.

I don't even know what I said at this point, if I'm being completely honest. I was *that* friend. The one who wants to speak to security to let them know everything is fine, but I probably shouldn't have been the one talking. And because I made the action of pushing myself in front of Bobby, hotel security called the police, claiming domestic violence abuse. The rest . . . Well, the rest you probably saw play out in the media.

I never in my life expected myself to be in a situation like this. To this day, I am still devastated and confused by what happened that night. So is everyone who knows me. As soon as I was released, Bobby and I booked a flight home. The moment we got to the airport I got a call from TMZ. Someone had tipped them off about my arrest. I was in shock. I hadn't even had enough time to process everything and my mug shot was floating around the internet. I couldn't wrap my brain around the media frenzy, so how was I supposed to answer questions about it?

Within minutes, my phone was flooded with texts and links to articles from various websites. It was, hands down, the most humiliating two days of my life. I wanted to hide under a rock and never come out. I was definitely grateful to have Bobby by my side. And our friends and families supported me, knowing the person the media was painting me to be couldn't be further from who I am. The words "domestic violence" did not describe me, Bobby, or our relationship. The press was saying I shoved Bobby, but anyone who sees us knows that isn't even possible. I'm 5'3". He's 6'7"! There was no way he'd move an inch no matter how much strength I used.

Even still, it was hard. I had never dealt with anything like this before. I felt immense guilt for Bobby, who didn't ask to date someone who was in the public eye, who was going to have his private life splashed all over the place. I felt terrible for him. I felt terrible for my kids, whom I had to drop off at school the next morning while getting dirty looks from the other parents. It was a mess. Online, people were commenting up a storm, assuming I was on drugs, had an alcohol problem, or party all the time. Even worse is that people were assuming Bobby and I must have a terrible, toxic relationship. For the first time, this couldn't be further from my truth! Anyone close to me knows none of those things are true, but I wanted *everyone* to know.

Most people never saw that Bobby was the one who was keeping my family in the loop when I was phone-less and helpless. He took on the responsibility of making sure all my loved ones knew I was okay, and on top of that, he wanted so badly to address the situation to let everyone know what the news was reporting couldn't have been further from the truth.

His eagerness and instinct to protect me showed me a different side to a partner I've never even thought to look for.

Despite everything, if I could take it all back, I wouldn't. I'm lucky that my friends and family know me well enough to stand by me, and their love and support really showed through this incident. I faced no judgment from my closest friends when

I was glad Bobby was there for me through all the craziness.

I got back and no one made me feel less than for a careless situation that happened in Vegas. I'm so grateful to know and love the people who have my back through everything. This incident has made all my relationships stronger.

Some bumps in the road may be bigger than others. And if you're reading this, I really pray your bumps are smaller than mine. But if they're not, you'll be just fine!

I have learned so much with everything I've been through. In the end, it's made me a stronger and better mother, girlfriend, daughter, and friend. The truth is, no one is perfect. Everyone makes mistakes, and we are going to continue to make mistakes for the rest of our lives. The best part about those mistakes is that you learn from them every time.

So there you have it: my love life in a nutshell. Reminiscing about all the things that happened in my past while writing this book has opened my eyes to so many things that I buried deep, deep down or even forgot about.

I am so grateful for my life now, but it took a long time to get over all the times I've been burned in the past—both privately and publicly. Now that I've taken the time to officially move forward, I wish I could say that I have my entire life put together and all figured out, but really . . . I'm not even close. It seems like, every day, I'm still learning something new.

Being with Bobby taught me a lot about being in a relationship in which both sides give equally. I had to be honest with myself and accept that effort from him, though. It wasn't easy at all at first. I thought maybe I was going crazy *because* we were so compatible. I was so used to being in relationships that were toxic, way too co-dependent, and emotionally taxing that I wasn't used to the patience that Bobby gave. I had to keep asking myself, *Is this normal?*

Going through life and being in relationships has made me realize how far I've come as a person. I've finally set boundaries in place when it comes to my needs, and I've finally started following my own advice when it comes to being in healthy, worthwhile relationships. There are still moments that bring about self-doubt, but I've learned to be patient with myself too.

With Kins and Char getting older, I now miss the moments when I could carry the both of them in my arms. I can't believe they are growing up so fast. They each truly have personalities of their own, parts of which I can already tell will be challenging when they get older.

Kins and Char have taught me everything I know when it comes to persevering, picking myself up when things are tough, and being the best version of myself. I always kind of laugh at comments on Instagram in which people say that my life looked "perfect" or that I was "mom goals." I love that sentiment, which encourages me to keep keeping it together for all the single moms who look to me for inspiration. But I just have to say that we all have good days . . . and we inevitably all have bad days, too. There are so many moments when I'm knee-deep in our dog Poppy's poop because it's been a mission to potty train her while Charlie is pouring hot wax from my favorite candle on the kitchen counter and Kinsley is crying because she fell running around in the house, and I'm on the verge of tears. But I just take deep breaths and

The two most important people to me in the world. I'm so lucky.

remember that these are the moments I'll miss. I'll miss sharing sweet laughs with a silly Charlie and nursing Kinsley's
knee with a giant bandage because she's just as dramatic as
her mom. No matter what the circumstances are in life, it'll
always be the three of us first before anything or anyone else.
I'm already anticipating the day when they try to date boys

in junior high because then I will *really* panic when they start breaking hearts (or vice versa).

If and when Kinsley and Charlie ask me about *The Bachelor*, I am going to tell them that it was the craziest yet most vulnerable thing I've ever done. It was the first time in a long time I made myself step out of my box. At that point, I hadn't gone out on a date in years and I had a hard, hard time being away from them. Mustering up that courage to go meet Ben and have Ben meet them (the first guy after their dad) was a whole learning experience in itself. More importantly, I am so grateful for the people I met on the show. They've become life-long friends and aunties of Kins and Char. Life is crazy—with or without *The Bachelor*—so I'm very fortunate to have gotten to experience something extraordinary like that. It really taught me to grow and took me out of my comfort zone. I can't imagine what life would have been like had I not received that phone call telling me I was chosen as a contestant.

One thing I know for sure is that you will never see me on *Bachelor in Paradise* again, and that (I think) my journey in Bachelor Nation has come to an end. I've gotten to know myself a lot better after the show, especially as a business-woman. I can only imagine myself working on creative projects like this book or my own clothing line or a self-owned brand. Never in a million years did I think that I would become an entrepreneur with ambitions or goals to have my own business, but I just needed the courage to believe in myself.

I hope one day I'll have one or two more babies running around while Kins and Char grow older and go to school (and forget about me!) and that we'll have a house with a yard where Poppy can run around freely, with backyard summer movie nights as a tradition in our home. I've learned over the years to just be thankful for everything that has come my way and, as long as my family is healthy and happy, there really isn't a need for more.

Throughout all the crazy messes I've managed to get myself in and out of, I'll still always look at roses as a symbol of love and how I'm so beyond blessed to be overflowing with it—even if it took me a while to accept it.

Epilogue: Letter to
My Daughters

Dear Kinsley and Charlie,

One day you'll be ready to take on the world of dating, and when that time comes, I want you to go into it prepared with a few pearls of wisdom I've gathered along the way.

While romance can be fun and fleeting, it is never more important than your relationships with your sister, your parents, your friends, or yourself. It's true that boyfriends come and go, but friendships last forever. Surround yourself with a tribe of positive, honest, loyal girlfriends. Lift each other up, cheer each other on, and come together when things aren't going so great. Sometimes people make their romantic relationships their whole world. When it doesn't work out, they feel empty and alone. With a tribe of incredible friends, you'll never feel alone.

When you're young, dating is all about figuring out what qualities you do and don't like. Always keep tabs on both so you can make choices that work best for you. Behaviors like selfishness, hot tempers, and impatience are qualities that don't work for me. I used to accept these behaviors in my past partners. I'd sweep things under the rug, but ultimately those relationships made me uncomfortable and unhappy, so I don't allow room in my life for them anymore. Instead I seek people who are kind to strangers, stay calm in stressful conditions, and always treat me with love. If someone ever makes you feel insecure in any way, if they make you feel unhappy, scared, or nervous, that is not okay. Those are not feelings of love. Feelings of love are stability, safety, happiness, and never being afraid of them or what they might do.

One day, you will have your heart broken to pieces. Actually, this will likely happen more than once. Heartbreak is the absolute hardest. The most important thing to remember is the intense pain you're experiencing is only temporary. And believe it or not, you're going to come out of it better and stronger, I promise. When your heart is hurting, lean on your friendships. Talk it out with them instead of holding it in. Let them get you out of the house. Go on walks, hikes, swims. Go shopping. Buy yourself a new pair of shoes (hopefully by this time these won't be light-up Skechers). Do whatever you can to shake it off. Know in your heart there is another relationship coming your way. Each time you start over with someone new it has a better chance to work out because you'll have learned something from your past.

When you decide to move in with a boyfriend or agree to get married, be 100 percent sure it is right for you. If you have even the slightest of doubts, hold off. Your instincts are always going to be right. Listen to them. If he loves you and you tell him you're not quite ready, he will wait. Each time I've been pressured into making a decision, it has never been the right one. The best way to know is to pay attention to how you feel.

When you're alone in a quiet space, ask
you're considering. If you feel knots in you
ness in your chest, those anxious feelings a
It might be best to hold off. If you feel elated
terflies in your stomach, this might be the righ
Remember, you're always supposed to feel go
about your decisions.

The honest truth is that you're going to mak
That's part of living! Rather than kicking yourself fo
when you should have gone right, skip the regrets ar
silver lining of every situation. There is always some
learn from every mistake.

You're both super loving, considerate, generous, fur
Kins, I love your sassy, big personality. If anyone ever tri
dull your sparkle, they're not your person. Char, I love h
much you love to be loved. Cuddles are your thing—make su
you find someone who wants to snuggle as much as you do
Never compromise who you are for anyone or anything.

I promise to follow my own advice, and I hope you will too.

Love forever,

Your Mom

Acknowledgments

Everyone knows behind every big project there's an army of people who made it all happen.

I'd like to thank, first and foremost, Bachelor Nation for accepting me and wanting to know more about my story. To my followers on social media, thank you for always supporting me in everything I share with you. It humbles me to know that I have such an amazing troupe of people who share advice with me and, in turn, appreciate what I have to say as well.

To my co-writer, Allie Kingsley Baker, working on this book together has been an enlightening and cathartic journey. Thank you for making the process fun and exciting! Thank you to my assistant, Tiffany Gomez, for supporting me through the project and wearing all the (cute) hats you do!

Special thanks to my book agent, Steve Troha; editor, Vy Tran; and the great BenBella team for all your hard work.

I appreciate my *Bachelor* franchise friends for contributing their funny first date stories to the book! Thanks for taking the time to share with us.

Shooting the cover of this book was a fun day I'll always remember! Thank you to the glam squad, Chrissy Rasmussen and Devon Duff, and photographer, Cory Tran, for delivering perfection. To my friends at Nightcap Clothing, thank you for the beautiful, cover-worthy dress.

To my family—my mom, dad, and sister, your unwavering support and quickness to bring me back to earth is something I'll always cherish.

And last, but certainly not least, Kinsley Elizabeth and Charlie Emma: You guys are my entire universe. I will spoil you, love you, smother you, cherish you, adore you, take care of you, be in love with you, and be the most embarrassing mom to you both always and forever. Thank you for teaching me all the lessons that I would never learn anywhere else. You guys are the best of everything I am.

About the Authors

Amanda Stanton is a single mother raising two beautiful girls, Kinsley Elizabeth and Charlie Emma, in Orange County, California. Before joining ABC's hit series *The Bachelor* and *Bachelor In Paradise*, Amanda was a full-time mom who hadn't been on a date in over five years.

© McCall and Nikki Ryan Photography

From her unique experiences on the dating shows, Amanda has received a crash course in relationships. She has developed a refreshing set of rules for what it takes to find the one—without losing oneself.

Allie Kingsley Baker is an author and lifestyle expert. Her novels, co-authored celebrity books, and screenplays are rooted in good humor and positivity. She lives in Los Angeles with her husband, Tony, and their baby girl, Kingsley Rose.

Photo by Cory Tran